Body Acceptance for Men

JADE NYX

ISBN: 9798357106919

DEDICATION

To you, you beautiful and wonderful human being.

Word From The Author

Hey Men, guess what! It isn't just you.

It really isn't. It's everyone. That super jacked dude? Him too. That skinny guy? Him. That mid sized guy? Him. We are all struggling and all thinking "If only I looked like this or that, then I would be happy, then I would be successful and I would matter". All of us are walking around pretending that we are the only ones who are struggling.

We are all suffering with our body image. No matter what body you are in. If you are thin, thick, disabled, male, female, andrygonous, poc, old or young. Whatever your body looks like, you are welcome here, this book is for the person, the soul, who needs it, not the body.

We can think positively about other people all we want but we are overly critical of ourselves and I am going to explain to you in detail as to why that isn't on you. It isn't your fault and it isn't just you.

You are not alone.

This is a journey you are about to embark on and it can be really scary unlearning everything and trying to work stuff out so I am here to cheer you on on your journey.

Everyone is different so the most important thing you need to do is leave your ego at the door, take a deep breath and listen, think about them for you and apply if you feel it's right for you.

If you're ready for change because you are so sick of being down, hating your body, feeling anxious socially because you are always adjusting your top to hide your body.

Then make a cup of tea my friend, it is time we become acquainted.

CONTENTS

INTRODUCTION

Hello handsome!

Thank you so much for taking a chance to change your life and successfully acquiring this book. I am Jade, it is great to meet you and I am going to be your guide through Body Acceptance. Like your own personal ghost friend but instead of haunting you or taking you on journeys into the past, present and future, I am going to be cheering you on and showing you the road I have already walked so when you start your journey, you won't trip over a boulder or get bitten by a rattlesnake. I hope this one paragraph sets the tone for the whole book because it only gets more eclectic from here.

This book is going to cover so many topics to help you reconnect with yourself and disconnect your body shape from your self worth. You may have noticed that there are both a regular version and a version for men. Full disclosure, the base content of the book is the same. The difference is male specific issues we cover and some of the wording is less floral which I think you would appreciate. This topic is already hard enough to face with the amount of bullying, harrassingment and expectation put on the media. Especially when there is a heavy lean on men not having mental health issues and just being told to man up instead of having feelings.

The media treats you like shit and I am sorry for that. Toxic masculinity is ruining your mental health and your relationship with your body. I can't change the world but I can create a more comfortable environment for you to open up and learn about body acceptance. And unlike razor blade companies, I haven't just put in blue packaging and doubled the price. I have rewritten a lot of this book with your issues in mind. Even though I am a lady (we will talk about that) and I haven't actually lived through the experiences you have. But I think I have a solution that can help you until a man actually steps in and starts speaking up. That could be you! You never know.

Firstly, settle a bet for me.

Doesn't Body Acceptance for Men sound like a trashy perfume ad? or not? Because I can't not hear a French woman whispering it in a faux-seductive voice.

Second thing you should probably know is that body acceptance, like most personal development, isn't a linear process. It isn't like going down a checklist and going:

Complimented myself, check!
Bought myself a water pistol, check!
Totally had a wash, check!
I must love myself now.

It is more like visiting a theme park that never closes. You enter the park and it is huge and there are loads of rides ranging from roller coasters to carousels and you get to choose which ones you want to ride. Everyone is different, not everyone loves death defying roller coasters and not everyone loves the tea cups but that is the glorious point of it.

We are all different. That is why theme parks are so diverse. You need to go on the rides that work for you and this book is just the map they hand you at the front gate so you can find the rides you want to ride.

You paid for your ticket, here is the map, it will point you in the direction of the ride and a small introduction to what it is and you have to go out in the real world and ride it.

And while enjoying this wondrous theme park, you are to be followed around by an annoying semi transparent ghost called Ghost Jade.

Much like any mascot, it is over the top, comically cartoonish and does dances every now and then to keep you entertained.

Did you ever play Rollercoaster Tycoon where to keep up customer morale, you had to hire entertainers to keep people happy when you built massive long queues? Ghost Jade is entertaining you while you are waiting in line to ride the coaster with 5 loops in.

Body Acceptance 101

You may be at that point in your life (like I was) where you can't even imagine loving your body. You have hated it for so long now it feels like an impossible task. You want to but you can't fathom how to and you see inspirational people talking "the talk" but never knowing how they walk "the walk".

Well my beautiful rainbowsarus, we start small. This book is the first step because before love, comes acceptance.

*Ghost Jade sings:
"First comes acceptance, then comes love, then comes dancing on the beach complimenting yourself and saying how you look fantastic and believing it"*

The point of this isn't to help you fall in love with you, that comes in time. The point is for you to accept your body for what it is. It is a tool for adventure. It is an organ that helps you experience life. (I will repeat this continuously throughout the book until it sinks in).

I want you to understand that you put too much pressure on your body to do things it simply isn't meant for. Your body's job is to keep you alive. Its job is to breathe and process food and spread blood around your blood tubes. Its job is to hear out for danger and see the wonders of a sunset in summer. Feel the first frost of winter under your fingertips. Taste a freshly baked cinnamon bun with cream cheese frosting and send your brain a lot of pleasure signals because it tastes so damn good.

Your body's job is **Not** to look a certain way to impress people. Your body is **Not** a vase.

It is funny isn't it. We are expected at all occasions to have our bodies be like a painting in a museum, flawless, pretty, perfect. But they are expected to work like the paint brush that painted it.

Your body is the paintbrush and your life is the canvas.

We live in a world where our bodies are treated like the paintings in the museum. We are supposed to keep them in perfect conditions. In frames, dim lighting so the paint never fades, locked in a vault and touched up so it never goes old. With people around us everyday, judging up, offering us tips on how to prevent peeling or fading. Offering interpretations on our lives and bodies through their own hipster filter, telling us who we are and what we mean.

Because if we don't look great, we have no value.

But like I said, just because the world is built that way, does not mean that it is true. You are more than just a body, you are an explosion of colour, energy and life. You are a paintbrush it is up to you to stop obsessing over the perfect painting and just get out there, be in the moment and create.

That is what body acceptance is.

You are handsome by the way, no matter what.

How do I want to approach this book?

Some of the best advice I ever heard was "take it slow, read a chapter, apply it to your life, then pick up the book and read the next when you are ready".

Everyone is different and learns differently but ideally I would like you to do one chapter a day maximum. Take the day to think about it, process it, apply it to your life. Maybe even discuss it with someone, although a lot of this content challenges pre existing beliefs and it can be hard when you are trying to let go of toxic beliefs about your body when you are surrounded by people who will argue for it.

Just a warning if you learn through discussion, take a pinch of salt with you into all discussions. *(and no, you cannot use it to get rid of Ghost Jade, she loves salt, she's not that type of ghost).*

Some people, I know you will want to blitz through this in a day and learn one thing and apply that to their life and that's your style you do you. I don't judge. I am both. Sometimes I like to read a whole book in a day then go back over and over again and get new takeaways each time.

But if you want to get the maximum amount of benefit from this, then take it slow. Overcoming a lot of old beliefs about yourself and your life will be really hard.

Finally, we need to address something before we even delve any further. I am going to call you beautiful, hey I might even call you pretty. You are going to have to get over that pretty fast. You are beautiful but I am sure the very idea of being called it made something in your brain cringe and roll around like a puppy in mud. You are beautiful, wonderful, smart, cool, brave and the OG. Deal with it. If you can't, maybe just skim through the final paragraphs at the end of each chapter.

And with that being said, let's get started and let's dive into the wonderful rollercoaster ride that is body acceptance.

Let the adventure begin.

Part One:

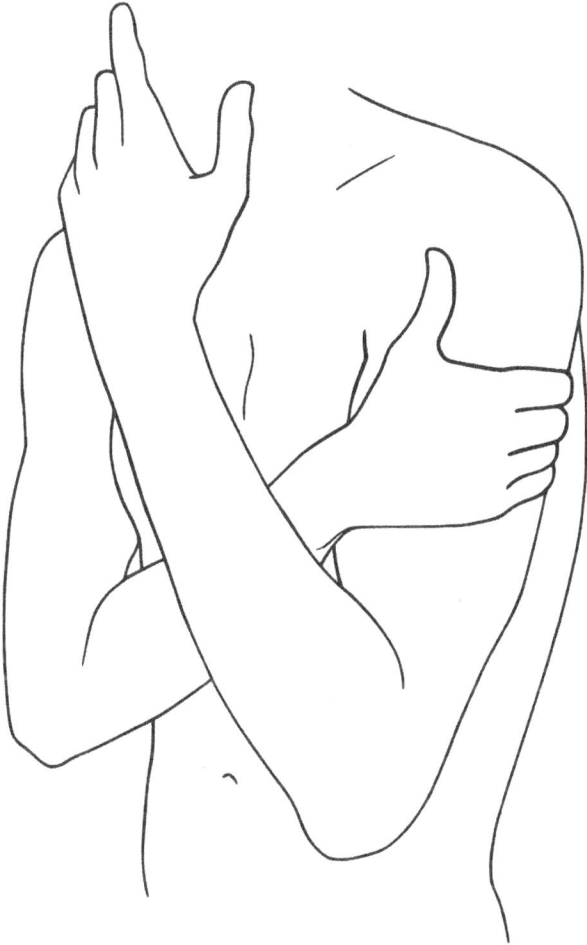

Elephant In The Room

MY BODY

Let's Address The Elephant In The Room. Hi guys, I am a lady. Is this ideal? No, cause I would rather a man talk to you about body issues because they have been through body issues from the male perspective. But also, there aren't a lot of male body positive activists floating around so here I am.

Let's clear one thing up right now, I love men. I think you are wonderful and brilliant and I love you. That is why I am writing this book (well a male version for you) because I hate seeing so many beautiful men in all bodies struggling with the unrelenting pressure and expectation put on you to perform and look a certain way. The Hollywood six pack, chiselled jaw Love Island Chad aesthetic that you are being pressured to conform to is sucking the life and soul out of you.

In this chapter, I mostly overcome body comparison so you can hear what I say without jumping into that comparative, competitive mindset but (and this is the best bit), we don't have that because we don't compare.

However, you will still have judgments about me and my body based on your own personal experiences with other people so if we just get over the whole gender and body thing and start treating me like a friend or more specifically, a Ghost friend, then we can actually start helping you heal your relationship with your body.

If you have seen me on social media or anywhere, Hello, I have a body, you are going to have thoughts and judgements about it.

If you have no idea what I look like, that is awesome, picture me as a ghost, however, that comes to you. Ideally, to me, it would be most hilarious if you pictured a little cartoon sheet with eye holes. That is how I picture me in your brain talking to you.

If you don't know me and the ghost thing isn't working for you, check out my IG @JadeNyx and I am sure there is a photo of me doing something ridiculous. Either way, I have a body so let's talk about it.

It is a small white body so who the fruitcakes am I to tell you about loving your body? I want to call out my thin white privilege ahead of time because if I don't you will always have that as an excuse in your head, to not listen to me.

You know **exactly** what I mean.

"Yeah but it is alright for her, she looks like that"

(I know because lord knows how many times I have said the same thing in my head and it is always the same in everyone's head and it loosely translates to:

It is alright for you because you are worthy of success, happiness and abundance but I am not so I will find a reason to prove this belief I have about myself."

Ya huh, called out)

For our first starting exercise (because accepting your body isn't reading a book and going "OH SNAP I LOVE ME", it is about doing the work day in day out).

I want you to have a look at my body because we need to address some reservations that you will have.

We are going to be talking about really difficult issues, we are going to be diving into the very lies you have been telling yourself.

That is why we are doing this exercise so that when I challenge you (and I will challenge your thinking and beliefs), you can't resort back to. "Oh but who is this girl in her small body telling me what's good", "She doesn't know. She hath not struggled as I have". In this perspective, this is technically true, I have no idea how it feels to struggle with male body issues but I am a firm believer that everybody has body issues. If you dig under all the gender and shapes, we are all fighting the same issues. Shame, hatred, fear all in different forms.

I have and I have my story. All you need to know is that I was once anxious, depressed, filled with self hate, constantly on a diet, never doing stuff I dreamed of doing cause I could do that when I was at the "ideal weight". Also I have been up and down the weight spectrum so when you think "yeah but she doesn't know how it feels to be plus sized or skinny", you'd be wrong.

I love my body, I do whatever the fruitcakes I want regardless of my weight and I love myself. I want that for you too.

We need to address some fundamentals here because if you are to learn anything, you have to overcome prejudices. I am not teaching you how to change your body into something you can love. I am talking about changing your view of how your body "should be" into something you should love. Without further ado, let's talk about my body.

Feel free to go have a snoop. When I filmed the original course for this, I went on camera, in a bikini and did a full show. But not everyone is a video person (personally, I am a massive book worm) so now if you have the opportunity to grab your phone, check out my social media.

Had a good look? Take some notes if you want, I don't mind. I want you to really let go and just write down everything that you think. The good, the bad, the ugly. I promise I won't judge.

Are you done? Great! What did you think? Feel free to take a few moments to really think about what you thought. No judgement or hate. Just really focus on it.

Guys normally have 2 reactions to my body.

1. "Oh my god, who does this pretty person think she is telling me about body acceptance, she doesn't know what I know, hasn't suffered as I have suffered. Skinny privilege at its best. A woman like that would never know what it is to be kind. Women like that have been assholes to me in the past"

2. "Oh my god, she is so fat, look at the size of her thighs. Like she's pretty I guess but like let's be honest, she's not skinny and skinny is beautiful. And WHO does she think she is being *so* confident looking like that? It is disgusting"

Other reaction include:

"Oh damn, she hot" *Ghost Jade blushes*

"Her eyes make her look like a witch"

"You're a nice person, the size of your body doesn't change how I feel about that" (These people are my people but remember no judgement, you thought what you thought.)

I just want you to think about what you thought. Did you go down the I am not good enough route? The trauma route? Or the Jade isn't a good enough route. Or did you have no reaction at all?

"Remember: You are not a collection of your thoughts"

It is true, I am all of these things, I am smaller and I am curvy and I am still hot (and so are you).

But see, all of these thoughts had nothing to do with me and everything to do with you.

Just take a moment to think about what you thought. Don't shame yourself or be disgusted by the bitchiness of your thoughts or the self hate of your thoughts, it isn't your fault, you have been conditioned to do this.

Think about how you reacted, was it rooted in self hate? Envy? Ego? Appreciation? Not everyone has a negative reaction but we want to talk about if you did and it is totally normal.

You can love someone with everything you have and still think thoughts like "well they got fat". We all do it, there is no person so *Evolved* that they don't make judgements about other bodies, it is human nature. Our opinions are built on our experiences and trauma. I cannot express how much this is built into our DNA, we are born to be judgy. Now let's slay some of those negative thoughts about my body with some facts.

Firstly, my body is not a representation of body acceptance, there is no one body type that is. Body acceptance means ALL BODIES ARE BEAUTIFUL. No matter what gender, age, sex, sexual orientation, ability, size, color, ethnicity or amount of limbs you have. We love ALL bodies. You don't have to be a woman to learn to accept and love your body. You don't have to change your body to learn to accept your body.

Secondly, don't shame yourself for thinking this way. This book is going to try and change those inner judgements and the way you look at your body. Which means we are going to face some dark uncomfortable thoughts that are mean. We are all mean inside, whether it is about other people or to ourselves. This is just human, you aren't perfect and that is okay.

Thirdly, none of what you thought about my body matters. It is my body, no one has a right to have an opinion on it but me. It's like having a kid, I am allowed to nurture and reprimand it but no one else does it. The reason I can sit here and not care what you think about my body, positive or negative, is because the only person whose opinion that is relevant to my body is mine. My body isn't a reflection of my self worth, we will get into this but how I look, isn't who I am. Being curvy doesn't make me lazy, being skinny doesn't mean I starve myself and being hot doesn't make me a bitch.

I can only represent body acceptance with the body I have. Currently there really are only 1 body type for men represented in mainstream media which if we are being honest, I don't quite fall into the category of. I would rock a beard though, don't you agree?

Skinny people get skinny shamed and curvy people get fat shamed. Me, I qualify for both but that isn't something I can control. I can't stop people hating me, I can only control myself and I choose to not shame anyone for their bodies.

Because it is a waste of my time.

Which is a nice segway into this little chestnut.

EVERYONE HAS BODY ISSUES.

Every **BODY** has body issues. Yes my beautiful men, most men you know have body issues, it is just no one is talking about it. To shatter the glass ceiling as well, the people with the biggest body issues are the ones who force themselves to conform to the male beautiful standard.

I have a lot of beautiful amazing hench male friends and they have just as many issues as my beautiful and amazing curvy male friends. No one is immune to being insecure and bullied about their body. Even people with the "perfect" body, they deal with abuse and shame all the time. I want to stop the endless need to body shame others but I can't because it all starts with each of us, making a conscious choice to change the way we think and the things we say. My dream really is for body shaming to be embarrassing so when someone does it in public, everyone cringes like "eww what a loser", that's my dream.

Because my smart and wonderful friend, the thing, pain is subjective. You could have ten men all lined up, all different body shapes, all different experiences and you can put them in the same situation and they would all experience pain differently. You could make a comment about a body and have it not affect them but it really affects someone in a different body. *(I hear your assumption that one body type is more targeted than others but you have no idea what someone else is going through, we are going to detach these assumptions we have about body shapes because everybody is different but more on that later).*

That is true of everyone and everything and it is so true of body acceptance. You can have different shaped bodies and you can have different pain or experiences.

I'm not devaluing your pain, we've all been through so much. That is why this book exists. I was anxious, depressed, always on a diet and I didn't do stuff that I really wanted to do because I wasn't "the right shape yet" and I wouldn't go do fun things.

I hated my body, my body was the enemy.

I wouldn't socialise. I wouldn't go out. I wouldn't travel. I once told myself that you can't go travelling by yourself because "you're not skinny enough. You're not attractive enough. You can't do that".

That "I can't do something because of the shape of my body" logic you have is going to ruin your life.

That attitude of I can't because of my body, it actually boggles my mind.

It hurts. It hurts to think like that. It hurts that you think like that now. Pain is subjective and we can't stop people being outwardly critical but we can change ourselves.

We can't control other people, we can't stop them judging your body, that isn't what this book is about. You can't control that, you can only control yourself. We want to stop you judging your body negatively. That is the goal and the starting point. When you embrace and love your body as it is, you inspire others to do the same and then we create a new world.

To conclude and give you a synopsis of what is to come, loving your body starts with you, not with changing your body shape.

There is no diet, product or item that can make you love your body. There is no outward validation from other people that can make you love your body.

There is no shape that you can make your body that will give you the things that you are looking for. Whether it's safety or acceptance or love or achievement or success, whatever it is you're looking for, it can't be found in a product or body goal.

It starts with you deciding that you love bodies of all sizes instead of shaming them for being skinny or fat and comparing yourself to people on the internet that have been photoshopped.

I know my whole life, I didn't do things, too unconfident to try because I didn't have that body type (you know the disney hero body type?). But here I am, doing what I love because your body doesn't stop you living your life, your lack of self esteem does. Self esteem that bullies, photoshopping and the media stole from you.

But, we are going to get that back. *Ghost Jade rolls a sword in her hand, raring for battle*

By the way, if that thought comes up "the small white person does not have the right to tell me how I should think or live my life", then that's your choice. Of course it is, you are more than welcome to ignore everything that I have to say. You have free will. This is like an informational roadmap or a guide book, it isn't a bible. If anything, go find a book, written by a dude. This is just sitting, waiting in the world for whoever needs it.

You can read it and you can take the lessons as you like but you don't have to do anything. I'm not here to tell you how to live your life. I'm here to give you the information that helped me live my best life.

I just wanted to share it so that other people could put on amazing and colourful swimwear and go to the beach and do whatever they wanted. Take selfies, dance, smile and act like a dumb idiot and enjoy their life and have fun, because that's really my goal in life, is to help people love themselves and have fun.

Here is the thing (and I truly believe this with every fibre of my being), I believe it is one of the most important things you will ever hear.

You are so mother fluffing worthy.

You and your body are amazing. You are beautiful, you are kind, interesting, smart, funny. You are passionate and fierce, even if you don't always feel it. You are inspirational. You are the most important person in your life and you are Awesome. With a capital A. You are exceptional and since I cannot walk into your house and throw you a "you are amazing I appreciate you" party for getting this book and reading, I am going to have to settle with telling you every chapter, how insanely epic you are.

Because you are. Insanely. Epic.

And you look fantastic today.

YOUR BODY

We can finally bring this back to **You**. Because you are learning to accept your body and now we have gotten mine out of the way, we need to focus on You. You are beautiful and your body is amazing. In this book, I want you to think about what I have said and think about your body as a separate entity.

Have you heard the quote "we don't have a soul, we are a soul. We happen to have a body" by C.S. Lewis? (Who knows if he really said it but I saw it on IG one day and loved it).

That is what I want you to think of yourself as. You are a soul. All those amazing things that make up you. Your skills, your compassions, your ferocity, your love. That is all your soul. Who you are is a soul, you just happen to inhabit a body.

Let's talk about that body because I want to tell you a story about dandelions. If you don't know they are a small yellow flower that grows wild in England, it is a very common flower. Its life cycle is fascinating, it flowers and then it turns into seeds with their own little inside out umbrellas. When we were children, we would pick them and blow the seeds off and they would fly into the world with wishes whispered into them.

I hear you, what does this have to do with my body? And what's with you and flowers? Well my friend, I will answer first, when I was young, the dandelion was my favourite flower. One day, my grandmother asked me what my favourite flower was and I told her that it was the majestic dandelion, that always reminded me of a lion's head and evolved into an explosion of adventure (I didn't say that but that's how I see it). She told me straight up that a dandelion was a weed, an ugly one at that and it couldn't be my favourite flower.

The next time I saw a dandelion, it looked different. It didn't bring me joy, it didn't remind me of a lion's head and I didn't appreciate its intricate petals and hardy attitude as it defiantly stares up at me, daring me to crush its spirit. My entire view of it had changed because someone pointed out that it wasn't as beautiful as I thought it was. It wasn't worthy of being called a flower, it was just a weed.

You can't tell me that you haven't had someone tell you that your body isn't good enough and suddenly you couldn't look at it the same way. Someone critiqued your ears, stomach, the way you smile, your bumps, wrinkles, eyes and toes.

When we were young, we didn't care what we looked like. Then one day, you were told you weren't good enough and that stuck with us. Maybe if we didn't live in a world that values beauty above anything else, kindness, courage, compassion, generosity, individually, intelligence. Maybe that comment could have been washed away with time. But it is too late, the belief was planted in your head and society, the media, people around you watered it until it bloomed out of control, bringing you nothing but pain, insecurity and sadness.

I ask you, which one is the weed? The majestic and hardy dandelion who feeds bunnies and transforms into a vessel for children to whisper wishes and dreams into the universe? Or the toxic and binding belief that your body isn't good enough because someone told you it wasn't.

If we didn't have beauty standards and all these expectations of what our bodies should look like, I wouldn't be writing this book. I'd be eating Khalua parfaits and dancing on the beach.

Your perception of your body is constructed around what other people think a body should look like. Constructed by generational trauma, the media, businesses and their ad campaigns that create reasons to be insecure so they can sell you their snake oil cure alls.

Your body is a dandelion and let me tell you why I love dandelions so much.

It's hardy, it survives and grows no matter what the winter has been like. It has so many layers, it's complex and intricate. The shade of yellow on the petals is the shade of happiness and abundance. It has a majestic aura about it in a humble sort of way. It transforms, it completely changes into something so incredibly beautiful and fun and adventurous. Sounds like you if you ask me.

Your body is so much more than just a majestic flower, your body is resilient, strong, transformative and sensational.

Take an actual moment to close your eyes and feel your body. I don't mean like pat yourself (you can if you want, wait till we get to sex and bodies) but I just mean close your eyes and bring your focus to your body. Your body is your home. It is your best friend. It is your ally in this world. You are lucky to have it. Just spend a few moments realising how amazing it is that you are alive right now. You have a body. It does its best to keep you alive. It isn't perfect but hey, it isn't supposed to be. Nothing is supposed to be perfect. Except maybe a puppy when it rolls onto its back and smiles at you, that is perfect.

Activity: Name 3 things about your body that you are grateful for.

I am grateful for how my body can heal, how useful fingers are and how I can taste cinnamon buns.

Isn't it amazing? It beats, it moves things around. Your body rocks just like you do. We are talking about your body but the reality is, it is only one part of you. You are a diamond and a diamond has more than one side. You are so innovative, compassionate, generous and hard working.

You rock and I appreciate you.

WHY DO YOU HATE YOUR BODY?

People love to tell me How they hate their body, but no one ever says Why.

Let's go right back to the start when someone insulted your body and took a chunk of your self-esteem. Ever since then we've been trying to get validation and acceptance back from other people, from the people who took it from you.

Let's be overdramatic. In the original book, I used a rose garden but (and this is going to be so stereotypical but we are going to do it) we are going to talk about Cars.

Picture your dream car. *Ghost Jade gets into a 1965 White Mustang*

Your beautiful dream car is sitting in your garage. Over time, people have waltzed into your garage and taken parts out of your car. It started with a wing mirror but then it was a wheel, spark plug, a rear wheel axle. Until there is just a shell left, just a rusting shell of a beautiful car. *Ghost Jade cries at her mustang named Destiny*

You feel heartbroken so you keep trying to go around and trying to get people to give you your parts back. I mean you know who "borrowed" them to use in their cars and likely will never return them.

Sometimes they give them back but they are broken, it no longer fits right, it's all rusted and useless. No matter how many parts you track

24

down, they are all in a state of disrepair. And then you start to think, well if people are stealing my car parts, I will just go steal some of other people. So the toxic cycle of shaming begins.

Here is the secret to self-esteem and self-confidence, you cannot get it from other people. Other people cannot give you your self-esteem and self-confidence back. They can give you a temporary ego boost, like sure it is nice when you get a part back but its rusted and eventually, you have to just get rid of it. Small victory, small ego boost but not there for longevity.

The person who broke you cannot be the person who fixes you. No matter what the movies tell you.

That is kind of true of everything. If you want to grow your self-esteem and self-confidence, you need to understand that self esteem and confidence comes from within. You need to rebuild your own heart because it isn't an irreplaceable gemstone, it is a majestic car. You have all the conditions to start over, you just have to get new parts and put them back in. Once the engine is turning and that amazing rumble starts, your self esteem and confidence will become limitless.

Yes, it takes time and it takes effort but we can do it and next time someone comes into your garage and tries to pinch all of your parts, hit them with the wrench.

Cars aside, I want to chat about why you hate your body.

Why do you hate your body? The most common reasons I hear is, "oh it's just fat, never losing weight, not good enough, it's sickly, pale, it's ugly, wonky, big in all the wrong places or it is too skinny, thick ears, wonky dong, small feet". The list is endless.

And all I hear is:

No One Will Love Me if I look like this. I cannot succeed if I look like this. I will not be accepted. I am not good enough.

And you are right, not everyone will love you for how you look. But there is no one on this planet, not even Chris Pratt who is beloved by all. You are not a God. You are a mortal human and that is okay. You cannot please everyone and that is not your job and it certainly isn't your body's job.

And I said not everyone, not NO ONE. Someone in your life loves you, accepts you and thinks you are good enough and I can assure you, I am one of those people. *Ghost Jade Cheers*

It is a crazy thought, I know, it's almost like you have a greater purpose on this earth than to look a certain way to please people. You aren't a vase. You are a strong, powerful, exceptional man and if people don't like the way you look, they can suck it. More on that later.

Here is my activity for you *Ghost Jade grabs a pen for you*

I want you to write down what you would get if you paid for that surgery, lost that weight, gained that bulk, had that extra limb returned to you. Whatever your hang up is. Like if Ghost Jade was a genie in your Mustang shaped teapot and I could with a snap of my fingers give you your perfect body, what would you get?

Acclaim? Success? Respect? Love? Safety? Protection? Attention? Free stuff? Sex? Promotions? Respect?

Here is one of my examples:

I wanted to lose weight and look like a fitness model because I want to be **respected**. I hated being underestimated in my fitness because my body has fat on it. This hath always vexed me.

In my experience with men, we lean to my friend Gary.

I wanted to gain weight and not be so skinny because then I could find someone to love me. Women don't like a skinny guy.

Write down what you would get because I want you to deal with these insecurities.

Let's take mine. I want respect. Respect is earned and sure, I could get it if I dedicated every waking hour to sculpting a perfect body but I would have to give up everything in my life.

Is that something I want? Or can I find respect for myself and not care what other people think of me or my body? It is my life and I am not a performing monkey.

I want to be perfect (ever the perfectionist), I can never be perfect but I can accept myself in my imperfection. A lot of these insecurities are things we need to face and accept that they are part of who we are.

By the way, there is never an end. No matter how hard you try, how perfect you are, you will always find new ways to change to be more. There is always more, prettier, skinner, curvier. It is an unbeatable battle. The only way to win is to get off the playing field.

For Gary, he just wanted to find someone to love him and see him for who he was. His body had nothing to do with it and cheering him on on his wedding day was a top moment in my life.

Face what you want to achieve by changing your body to be "beautiful" and then deal with it.

Face it and accept that this is part of who you are and you can reign it in. I have to reign in my perfectionism and my desire for glory. It isn't always easy. Trust me. But it takes the pressure off your body. It's not your body's fault you want to be loved.

This is all going to change and happen when you ask yourself, what is it that you truly want in life? Who are you and what do you want? To travel? Be a parent? Start a business? What is it that you would do if your body wasn't "holding you back"? Because when you let go of this idea, you can divert all this energy you are wasting on obsessing about your body shape and not being good enough to your actual dreams.

Weight loss or gain, wishing you looked younger and changing your body will rarely bring you the thing you truly seek. Don't worry about it and focus on accepting your body for how it is. Not for how it isn't enough.

Hating your beautiful body isn't going to get you the things you want in life and you deserve the things you want in life. It is okay to be ambitious and want things for yourself. You are gorgeous, talented, wild and interesting. You deserve to be happy and you deserve the world and yes, I believe that 100%. I don't lie, I am terrible at it so I gave up that a long time ago.

Happiness isn't found in having, it's in just being.

This is one of my favourite quotes of all time. Having the perfect body isn't happiness, living your life as it is just being, is where happiness can be found. I love this quote because I find it really beautiful. I really think it applies to bodies because having the perfect body isn't happiness. Just being, just existing in your body is happiness.

Which brings us back to the most important question, what do you really, really want from your life?

It is time to face those insecurities. Face that thing that you want. Find what parts of your heart have been taken out by other people and focus on growing them.

Focus on healing those insecurities that you have. By making yourself feel confident, secure and safe, you will heal your relationship with your body. *I did tell you. I told you you were going deep. Right in the author's note I warned you.*

We've had self-esteem and self love taken away.
We need to regrow it.
What is it that you want from your life? What do you want to achieve in your lifetime?
Do you want to be a parent?
Do you want to talk business?
Do you want to go travelling?
Do you want to buy a cabin in the woods and live by yourself with ten dogs?
Do you want to grow the world's most impressive moustache?

By healing your relationship with your body, you will suddenly find that you're not obsessing, constantly doubting yourself or spending all of your mental energy focusing on why you hate your body.

When you heal you'll actually have all this space, energy and time to focus on the things that you do want from your life.

This book exists because I healed my relationship with my body and I had all this free time and I was like "you know, I really fancy doing, I really fancy helping other people get to this place of happiness".

Instead of sitting around thinking "oh my barnacles, I should be on a diet and obsessing over what I'm eating" or "what am I wearing today, the same old clothes because there is no point in buying new clothes, I will lose weight soon right? When I lose weight, then I can buy new clothes, I am on the brink of change...right?".

Wrong. By overcoming these insecurities you have you can explore new areas of yourself and your life.

When I healed my relationship with my body, I was able to go travelling, start businesses, do all this crazy, insane stuff I would never have done if I still hated my body.

All bodies are meant to be different, there isn't meant to be one type of beautiful. I will refer to your body as several different things, plants, cars, bats in a belfry but your body is like a car, there are loads of different models but they all get you from A to B. But the most important thing I need to highlight is that you can do anything you want. You have the ability to do anything regardless of the shape of your body. The only thing stopping you is your belief that you can't because of your body shape. Not your body itself.

Your body is amazing, you are amazing. You are so much more than your body. Your life isn't defined by how you look, it is defined by what you do with your life. You are creative, smart, wild, rambunctious, kind, passionate and interesting. You have such an amazing life to live and so many wonderful things to do and they all have nothing to do with your body shape.

ADVENTURE

This will be short and sweet because we want to cover one point and one point alone and that is. Your body is a tool for adventure.

Your body is not an ornament or a piece of artwork. It is a functional tool. It is a car that takes you places. It is a ladder that helps you acquire the delicious cookie jar. It is a super computer. It is the hammer that you construct shelves with. It is a tool you use to achieve your goals.

Your body is a tool to experience life with.

We have to, **HAVE TO**, disconnect your body with your self worth.

I understand the desire to look fierce and sassy but we need to disconnect that idea of If I Look A Certain Way I Will Be Attractive And Therefore Worthy. You are worthy regardless of what you look like.

Your body, your looks, your physical form isn't a reflection of who you are. Do you want to die and at your funeral people go, "Oh yeah, they were really pretty, really dedicated to looking attractive"? Or do you want them to say "Oh yeah they were kind, strong, brave, powerful, smart, wild, accomplished, funny, brilliant, artistic, pragmatic".

Because no matter how much you try, they are always going to default to the latter anyway. No one cares what you look like, they only care about you.

Your body is a vehicle to drive your way through your life. There are so many different types of cars and they all serve different purposes. Some of us drive Renault Clios covered in sand and dog hair and some of us drive polished Ferraris. They are technically cars, their purpose is the same, to move you from one place to another. The only difference is their perceived value, I say perceived because we assign value to it. If it was a zombie apocalypse, I can assure you, you wouldn't want a Ferrari, you would want a tank. In a zombie apocalypse, a Ferrari would be useless, we assign a different value to it. The point of this example is to highlight that although cars have different purposes (because we all live different lives), they do a job. They take you from destination A to destination B. They aren't supposed to sit in your garage and look pretty and they are all different. Just like bodies. If we all drove around in matte blue Priuses, it would be a very dull world.

If you want to dedicate your life attempting to be the epitome of beauty then I say go ahead. Seriously. It's your life. If you want to be a pristine polished Ferrari, do it. There's nothing wrong with doing something you want to do, Ghost Jade will cheer you on. But I will warn you, beauty is in the eye of the beholder and it is ever changing. You could be beautiful one day and then hideous the next, Society is cruel that way. Society profits on our self hatred. If we hate, we can buy products to cure all our indiscretions.

You are more than just your looks. You are beautiful, compassionate, artistic and brave. You look exceptionally beautiful regardless of what other people think.

You are more than just society's opinion of your body. You are so much more than that. Your body is just a tool so you can do all the amazing things you are going to accomplish. Climbing Everest, having children, opening a really tough pickle jar and showing up to some man who thinks you're weak because you are smaller than him. Your actions and accomplishments are who you are and where your worth stands.

There are so many cool things you can do with your body.

Once you start seeing the fact that your body is just a tool, you can start going on the beach and not worrying so much what people think of the shape of your body because your body isn't there to be objectified like artwork.

Your body is there to experience how it feels to have the waves wash over you, the sand between your toes and how annoying it is when you stand on a prickly shell.

Your body is worthy no matter what. It is your actions that define you so make sure you live with intention. Decide who you want to be and act on it and show your body the kindness it has needed since the day someone made you feel unworthy because of how you look.

Let's talk about the unrelenting power of intention.

Your life is a creation of your reality that is based on your ideas and beliefs. That is why two people can watch the same things and have vastly different views. Two people could look at a Ferrari and one could say "Oh my, what a nice car" and the other could go "Not for me, I prefer my cars to be eco friendly and electric".

Ghost Jade revs her Mustang

Your beliefs are what make you, you, but these can sometimes get you into trouble. Which is where the power of intention can drastically change your attitude toward your life.

If you have the belief that you are fat and therefore worthless, your brain will find reasons to back up that belief system. However, this is an automated process. You had this belief installed by someone else when you were young (stomped on your dandelion if you will). It sucks but it's there and your brain has been reinforcing that belief ever since.

However, that doesn't make it true. If you have a belief that you are unworthy, nor good enough, a loser, destined to fail. Just because you have that belief, doesn't make it true. It just means your perception of reality is skewed to support that belief system.

But we can change that right now with the power of intention. The power of intention setting can change your experience of living. You can set an intention to be the opposite of your belief and it can build up a counter belief and change your perception of reality. All you need to do is choose it and question the negative.

If you live more intentionally and appreciate the fact that you have the luxury of still being here, on this wonderful planet and have the opportunity to grow and work on your goals and find your purpose.

Let's talk about how. What does it mean to live intentionally?

Here is something I love:

If you feel: Depressed, angry, hateful, sad, regretful or ask "why me"? You are living in the past.

If you feel: Inner peace, bliss, joy, love, calm, content, grounded and connected to the now, you live in the present.

If you feel: Anxious, pressured, stressed, overthinking and plagued with what ifs, you live in the future.

Did you relate to one of those? I know I spent a lot of my life afraid and living in the future and depressed living in the past.

The power of intention setting can change your experience of living.

If you want to be more positive, set the intention to be more positive. Which means when negativity comes knocking, you will be brought back to that intention of questioning it and trying to find a positive.

Your entire life changing to be happy starts with you deciding that you don't want to be hateful. You don't want to spend your days hating your body and watching content that makes you feel more insecure and down on yourself. It starts with you setting the intention to consume positive content, the intention of ditching negativity out of your life and the intention to be proactive in what you believe in.

Activity: Pick The Word

I love this activity, I do it weekly. I pick a word, an adjective about how I intend to approach the week. It can be Brave, Productive or Kind, Rest, Chill Out. Pick a word that represents how you want to face the world today. Forgiveness, compassion, love are great ones for helping you with your body. Patience is always another one because people will test your patience to no end.

Your body is a very handsome looking tool by the way. You have a great butt and a wonderful smile.

PERMISSION

This is short because I am here with one purpose and that is permission.

I am giving **YOU** permission to love your body. It is probably that no one has ever told you that you can love your body, no matter what it looks like. Crazy. I know. I never had that, society and magazine covers constantly tell us that we shouldn't because we should look like this guy *Insert beautiful celebrity* *Ghost Jade does a blue steel pose*
And then we flip the page and we see:
"LOOK AT THE BELLY ON HIM, SO FAT, DISGRACE!"
It's the same person.

You don't have to listen to that toxic standard of beauty. The Hollywood Chad Persona. You have the power to decide that you are beautiful, no one can give that to you.

You have to fight for it yourself.

You have a choice to give yourself permission.
To not be perfect.
To not look like the heavily photoshopped images on social media, in magazines and in any form of media.
To just have a normal body.
To just be you.
To accept your body as it is, no changes are required.

And you have the choice to give yourself permission to know you don't have to and no matter what your body looks like, it is good enough.

Society loves to tell you that it isn't but you can choose to ignore them and choose to focus on the good enough instead of the not good enough.

And if you don't feel up to it, here is me, "Hi I am Jade, I am giving you permission to love your body because you are allowed too and you should. It is stupid not to you and you my friend, are not stupid". *Ghost Jade agrees*

Activity for you:
Sit down and just give yourself permission. Take a deep breath and really think about it. Make a conscious effort and do whatever you need to do.

If you want to write it down, declare it on social media, do a spell, buy yourself a new pair of 'I give myself permission pants'. Whatever comes naturally to you. Do it. Give yourself permission to accept your body as it is.

You are epic and you can have anything you want in life. You are patient and accepting and to be honest, you have gotten this far through this book, you have to be. You have a wonderful laugh and the way you put care into the things you love is inspirational.

Part Two:

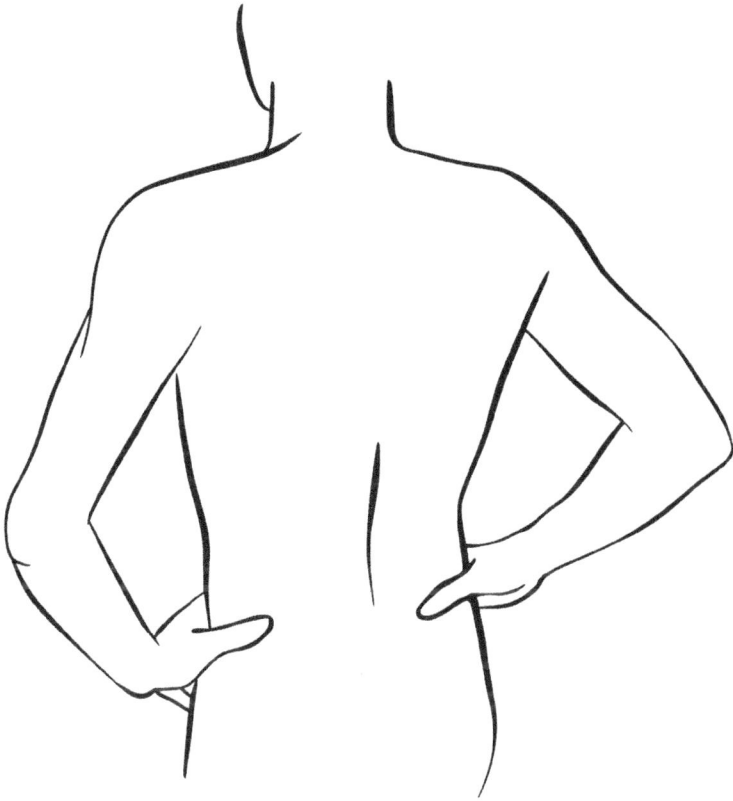

All About You

INNER THOUGHTS

I want to chat to you today about Your Inner Critic. AKA the world's biggest Dongbasket. Pardon my french.

The way we talk to ourselves Matters. Did you know that plants respond to positive and negative intentions? A school ran a test once, two identical plants in the school lobby, same exact watering, conditions etc and the students were encouraged to insult one and praise another. Want to guess what happened? The praised plant thrived. The insulted plants withered. This has been proven over and over again. You, my friend, are a plant with a rose bush for a heart.

The Way We Talk To Ourselves Matters

Don't believe me, get a plant and test it.

We all have one, a hate filled internal monologue, it's a dick and there is nothing wrong with you, you aren't the only person that has one. We all have negative Ned in our heads, moaning away (or critical Clarence) making sure that you feel worthless at every step.

It is like when you are in your garage with your dream car *Ghost Jade Revs the mustang* polishing the chassy, there is another person walking around criticising the types of cars you like and saying how you totally should have a Ferrari instead.

Ghost Jade grumbles "what do they know, my Mustang runs circles around their Ferrari"

Let's start with some science.

Fun Fact Number One. As humans, we are built to survive, we are animals after all and one of our survival instincts is to search for danger, assess, be critical and fight or flight. Since we don't fight tigers in the rain forests anymore, our instincts have evolved into new threats which are social and emotional.

Have you ever noticed how you are drawn to all newspaper article headlines that are always rooted in over the top life threatening fear? That is because of the negative bias in your head. That is your danger, assessing and critical fight and flight response in your brain working.

The negative bias in our head is there to protect us from danger. By being critical of ourselves, we are protecting ourselves because if someone criticises us, that's nothing new, we do that all day, the pain is less. As a result, we continue to be critical.

Fun Fact Number Two. Humans are a community based animal, we need to be accepted by the tribe. In olden times, we had to conform to the tribe's ideals because if we didn't and we lost favour, we would literally be kicked out and thrown into the wild to be subjected to the circle of life aka eaten by lions, falling down a crevice or just die from exposure to the elements.

Consequently, it is always in our best interests to stick with the pack and we still have that mentality. This means, biologically, we have a desire to get approval from people, which is why we have developed these narratives about ourselves. Society has crafted this narrative and we want to conform to stay safe.

For example, Society says "If you look like this, you will be attractive" and we go "Of course, it makes sense, don't want to not be attractive so yes of course". Like the weirdest game of Simon Says ever.

Society (aka the tribe) however, has created a lot of weird and unusual expectations of bodies and in our desire to conform to society's expectation of what our body should be, we can't. Which mean we use our inner narrative (that fear soaked negative bias) to torture ourselves about not being good enough because as long as we are trying to conform we are safe right? ... Right?

But here is a secret and a reason as to why we should be rebels.

We give power to what we give attention too

What we focus on, we give attention to, we give power too. Think about it, if you water a plant, it grows right? If you stop watering it, it withers and dies. If you are focusing on the positive, the positive thoughts will thrive because you are watering them. If you are sitting thinking about how you can do this and it's scary but you've overcome so much and you can do this; you are way more likely to do it than if you were sat thinking about all the times that you have failed in your life. As I have said, you and your thoughts are like a pot plant.

It's kinda like when you were a child and you are given five pounds to spend on anything you want.

You buy sweets or you buy a book, one is clearly going to be better than the other but most of the time, we will buy the sweets because we are children and sweets are delicious.

Well in a way, we still are making that choice everyday. It's easier to think negative thoughts (buy sweets) because we are biologically programmed to do so with our survival instincts and socially, we were raised to be grumpy geese by other negative minded people (adults love sweets too). It is built into us to choose sweets. Also fun fact, we are biologically programmed to conserve energy and be lazy so we will always pick the easier option.

We are still being given that five pounds everyday except now we aren't children anymore, we choose what to spend it on. Maybe it is time to stop buying sweets and start buying books.

Because let's be real and adult here, if you are constantly thinking about how fat/ skinny/ ugly/ not good enough you are, your brain and body will respond to reinforce that belief which leads me to your belief system and your reticular activating system. *Ghost Jade is excited to talk about science*

Your belief system is a system of values and beliefs that were drilled into you when you were young and you still hold those values. Remember the majestic and awesome dandelion? If you grew up in a home where a parental figure made you feel worthless on a frequent basis, you have the belief that you are worthless. A more general example is if when you are young (this happened to me), my brother would tell me I was fat and stupid, as a result, I believed it and my behaviour adapted accordingly, I ate more and didn't pay attention in school. He implanted a belief in me and I reinforced it.

Lets break this down in a classically stupid and hilarious way.

I want you to think of your brain as two people working on a team project. You have the idea person (we shall name them Velma), it's Velma's job to think. Velma's job is to come up with thoughts and present them to the team. Their partner, (whom we shall name Patrick), it is their job is to come up with proof to back up Velma's theories and thoughts. Their job is to prove that Velma's wild and insane theories are in fact true by finding overwhelming evidence to support that nature. It doesn't matter what Velma's thoughts are, it doesn't matter if Velma thinks the Queen of England was a lizard, Patrick will find evidence to support that.

Or since we have a plant theme going, they are kind of like gardeners, Velma plants the seed and it is Patrick's job to water and take care of it to make sure it thrives and they are very good gardeners.

We look for things that support our belief system, for example, if we believe we are fat, we will look for things that support and reinforce that belief system. You will look for people who are smaller and go "look, they are smaller, therefore, I am not good enough". Or you will find media articles that reinforce your belief and you will ignore all contradictory information because your brain is wired to build up preexisting beliefs.

Velma presented the theory because they thought it or were shamed into thinking it and Patricks been hard at work proving it right.

What we want to do is identify and remove those negative beliefs (or Velma's theories, if you will) from your head because although they are deeply ingrained, they are also not true.

We want to remove the negative beliefs you have about yourself that have been implanted in your head and replace it with a healthy alternative that can only benefit you because your negative beliefs are only hindering you, they aren't protecting you.

We want to plant new beliefs that are positive about your body. If you want to sit around thinking about how much you hate your body, Patrick will water that plant. But if you want to change and learn to love your body and make actual changes, you need to tell Velma what your new belief is and make sure that V and P are focused on that. A really good way to do that is through key phrases and intentions.

This whole section in this book is about changing your life in order to make sure that you live in a world that automates the growing process so that you don't have to constantly remind yourself and refocus on positive thoughts. As we have established with our negative bias, it requires effort to think positive. Positive thinking is a habit cultivated through time.

To loop back around, to "we give power to what we give attention to". The more we focus on Velma's thoughts, the more Patrick is going to research and find proof that it is real. They are going to keep loading up the project file until it's an overflowing file cabinet taking up more space in your brain and life. Your head is filled with overflowing filing cabinets of negative beliefs. Or in the garden, Patrick is going to continue watering the new plant until it is this huge untackleable, out of control vine that takes over most of the garden, stealing the light and sucking the life out of all the other plants. We need to start saying no to the negative thoughts in your head and start moving forward and reprogramming your mind to be more positive. The great news is Velma and Patrick are freelance.

Velma and Patrick aren't the enemy here, they (like the rest of your body) are tools. They are just the hammer, you decide where to hit. You can aim for the nail or you can hit yourself in the hand. The choice is yours.

Which brings us to an exercise that I like to do. I call it: **Can it Clarence** but you can name it whatever you want.

The idea is to separate the negative narrative in your head by giving it its own persona and identity. Create it as another person (like we have done for Velma and Patrick) and we are going to create a positive voice as well. This isn't an angel and devil on your shoulder kind of deal, we aren't talking about morality, we are talking about that self bullying narrative voice in your head and having your own personal Ghost Jade, your personal cheerleader who punches Clarence in the face for insulting you.

Anyway, you need to give an identity to Clarence.

Give it a name (Ned for example or Old Me, Beryl, Lucifer, Cabbage). There are endless choices, just make sure you pick something that is fun to shout shut up to.

Then when you hear those thoughts, popping up in the back of your mind, tell you that you aren't good enough, your body isn't good enough. Tell it to shut up Nancy. Can it Clarence!

44

Silencio Bruno! You hear me?
You can even use the phrase Silencio Bruno!

When the voices come knocking around in your garden, tell them to fruitcake off.

I often use the phrase "we don't think like that anymore" and slam the door on it.
Or I politely invite Ned to take an extended vacation the fork away from me.

Whatever works for you, practice identifying the negative narrative in your head, separate it, realise it isn't the truth, it is conditioning, it's just an opinion based on lies. You can redirect Patricks hard working skill set onto a more worthy cause.

Use a key phrase, use a set intention, use whatever tool you want to use to redirect yours and Velma's attention onto the new positive belief you want to have about your body.

Remember, you are biologically wired to think negatively, as a result, it is easier to focus on the negatives than the positives but you have the choice everyday to wake up and fight. Say "Heckkin No, Fork You".

You are the one who is saying this stuff, you are Velma. No one else is to blame but you. Sure someone else planted the seeds in your garden for your negative belief plant to grow but that is out of your control. You can't turn the clock back, you can only move forward, stop watering the plant (and you should stop watering the plant). Send Velma and Patrick off to another department to work on the I LOVE ME project instead. Let that obnoxious and all encompassing plant die from neglect.

Now we have talked about the metaphorical devil you know, let's talk about the angel.

Utilising Ghost Jade

The concept of the Ghost Jade is to be a friend you have that haunts you with positive thoughts and vibes. Occasionally, it pops up and goes "wow doesn't that flower look nice" or "Tut Tut, sounds like rain" and you are caught up in Winnie the Pooh nostalgia. The voice we are looking for is the one that whispers good things in your head that make you smile. That is the voice we want to hand a megaphone too. During this book, Ghost Jade has been fulfilling this role, that is her job. I am your external friend who is telling you, you are gosh darn it worth a damn.

But here is the thing, Ghost Jade can be anyone. That's kind of the point of the Ghost.

You get to pick a face and voice for your positive cheerleader, it just has to be someone who makes you feel happy, loved and understood.

You are welcome to use me as a ghost in whatever form you like. You can choose a younger you, when you were 7 and you wore sandals and Thomas the tank engine shirts.
You can pick your favourite tv character, you can pick yoda. There is no one stopping you.

It can be someone who inspires you and makes you feel great about yourself. It has to be someone you can see saying positive things about you because (and hear me out) Han Solo is very cool. But could you picture Han Solo reminding you that you are attractive no matter what body shape you are, you are loved and valued and you are worth a damn?

Han Solo is cool but make sure you pick someone who you can see supporting you, not telling you to "man up" because that is just counter productive.

Personally, my Ghost Jade isn't my own voice, it's a tv character that I really love. They take up a little space in my mind and when a negative thought comes wandering into my conscious brain, their voice pipes up and they scare it off.

This battle is all in your mind, we might as well make it fun, like customising your phone!

The only thing I have found is that it can be easy to take a character and apply it to your brain. I mean I can't stop you, you can use Megan Fox if you want too but just remember, that you are creating an alternate character for them, like fan fiction. However, just remember your fan fiction isn't canon so you can't get mad when people don't act like you want them too. It feels stupid and patronising to say outloud but we all do it. We hear music, we relate to it, we create this idea of who this artist is in your head and then you are frustrated when the artist does things we don't agree with. The whole separating the artists and art thing. Anyway, let's move on!

Ghost Jade "That was WAY too many Star Wars reference for someone who hasn't watched them all"

Before you adventure off further into this book where I will try to convince you to try something fun, I have an activity for you.

I want you to write down myths that you have about your body and then you basically dispel them.

Some people like to think it but I like to identity and cast out these stupid myths about my body.

Things like:

Fat is bad, My body isn't good enough, I should lose weight to be healthy. *Ghost Jade "If this confuses you, wait till you get to the food section, it's going to be a duzy"*

Write down these inner bad thoughts you have had about your body and create counter arguments.

Fat is bad. *No it isn't, it's essential for survival and there is nothing wrong with having fat.*

Skinny is unattractive. *That is not true at all, you are very attractive. Skinny guys hook up with attractive people all the time. Two Words. 10th Doctor.*

My body isn't good enough. *My body is perfect as it is, it's job isn't to conform to unrealistic beauty standards.*

I should lose weight to be healthy. *I don't need to change my body in order to be healthy. I can be healthy at any size.*

And then if you feel like it, you write down all the things you hate about yourself and burn it because you don't believe in those toxic beliefs anymore. They aren't true.

Your brain may feel like it's the enemy sometimes but your brain is amazing. It is so smart, almost too smart but it's creative and chaotic but in the best way. The thing is your brain loves you too, your whole body does. You are gorgeous and appreciated and it is time for you to start cheering for yourself. That seems like a scary concept but you are awesome and nothing back actually happens when you start cheering for yourself. It isn't arrogant to love yourself, only good things happen when you start to cheer for you.

EXERCISE

Nothing can help you connect with your body like fitness. Pure physical power.

You may be somewhere on the fitness spectrum, maybe you never tried it, maybe you hate it, maybe you regularly train.

I want to talk about the benefits of exercise and why it's so important to enjoy exercise rather than just training to look a certain way.

How is exercise good for body acceptance?

Your body is built to move. You are an animal that is built to run, move, climb, dance (not just gyrating in the clubs boys). That is one of the primary functions as a human being and as a result, your body rewards you.

Doing exercises releases these chemicals in your brain:

Endorphin: Endorphins mask physical pain and promote feelings of happiness.

Dopamine: Dopamine boosts our mood and makes us feel great. It contributes to the feeling of accomplishment and elation from completing a task, achieving a goal, or winning in a game.

Serotonin: Serotonin boosts our confidence and makes us feel awesome. It also supports a sense of pride, status, and gratitude.

Oxytocin: Invokes feelings of love and loyalty. This chemical drives us to be around people we like and trust. Oxytocin is produced through human touch and acts of kindness or generosity.

Biologically speaking, our bodies need food to survive which means we need positive reinforcement. Exercising = Finding Food. Which means, our bodies reward us for exercising to encourage us to do it again.

By getting moving, you get that heart rate up and then you can use it to your advantage to handle stress, improve your mood, increase your confidence and help you feel more abundant and in love with your body and your life.

I once saw a quote that said "Exercise is the most underused antidepressant of all time" and that really struck a chord with me because that really was true for me. I was in a really low place and exercise brought me back from the brink. Personally, I find it much easier to love yourself and your body when you have all these chemicals glowing through your brain. Doesn't mean everyone does but for me, it's a cornerstone of it.

Another reason exercise can be so important to improving your relationship with your body is accomplishment. If you have a job where you don't get that feeling of accomplishment or growth or your life feels stagnant. The greatest thing about fitness is that you get better every time and fast. You get to see progress happening and that can be a really rewarding thing, not just for your body image but for your mental health and life in general. We aren't built to stagnate, we are built to adventure.

Exercise is also a celebration of your body. It is strong and versatile and moving it like it is designed to do is a great way to celebrate how amazing it is. You may not have found an exercise you like yet in your life or maybe you have. But now is the best time for you to reconnect with exercise.

I want to say this because this was always my fitness hang up and something years at Crossfit has taught me. *Ghost Jade "Of course I have to bring up crossfit, it is in the code, you have to talk about it! #itsTotallyaCult! Send Help!"*

Literally, no one cares what you are doing.

No one is sitting judging you.
No one thinks you are a fat tub of lard rolling on a treadmill.
No one thinks you are too skinny to lift that weight.
No one cares.

You get three reactions if someone happens to care:
1. People cheer you on for training at all.
2. People are sat worrying about what you think of them
3. People have those judgy negative thoughts but we don't care because the opinions we have discussed are not important. A lion does not care about the opinions of sheep and you, my amazing soul, are a lion.

And if you do get some body shaming butthole who bullies you, find another and more positive environment or report them. *Ghost Jade is a total nark*

If they come up to you and say, "hey you reported me!", you can tell them how they have made you feel and that body shaming attitudes are outdated and they won't find true happiness as they are. Then offer them more information on how they can grow as a person.

Or just blame Ghost Jade (seriously, just blame a ghost, it's hilarious) and Ghost Jade will flip them off for you.

But again, we aren't here to talk about controlling other people. We can't control what we can't control. We focus on what we can control. Us.

Don't let fear of judgement stop you from embracing fitness and pick something you really want to do. Dance classes. Zumba, swimming, pilates, weight lifting, youtube workouts, Muay Thai. I am not gonna lie to you, it can be scary and intimidating being a newbie to a class, if you have ever walked into a weightlifting session and just the most hench dude in existence is there coaching... I feel you, I really do. But, don't let that stop you because they literally don't care about you because here is the secret. The big ol' secret that everyone is keeping from you.

THEY ARE TOO BUSY WORRYING ABOUT WHAT YOU THINK OF THEM

They are sitting, "oh god do you think they think I am hot, I am good enough, what if they think blah blah".

No one cares. Like I said right at the start, you are not alone. Get over it and try a weird class. If you don't like it, try something else.

Now let's take a cute but casual segway into the world of adventure.

Because let's be real, not everyone likes working out. Not everyone enjoys going to the gym or running or exercise in general. Remember this is your life, I don't know what is best for you, only you do. That is why this book is a pick and mix.

There are other ways that you can get some dopamine into your system without having to fall on your face after attempting a handstand push up (yeah, those are actually a thing, people do them). First and foremost, it is just to get outside.

Get into Nature. Go for a walk, a swim. Do a cold sea dip (or if you have the luxury, a regular non cold sea dip), dance on the beach, do some gardening, walk a dog. Play Pooh sticks at a river. Nature is the most effective way to feel better. I love walking around a forest, it sucks negativity out of you like a hoover. If you don't want to work out, that is fine but every single day, especially if you are really committed to accepting your body, spend 5-10 minutes a day in some form of nature.

You have a body. Move it. Connect with it. If you don't know where to start, try yoga. It's slow, easy and all about body connection (it isn't for everyone but then what is). Find your thing and embrace it and once you do let go of the fear of judgement and have some fun, you will never want to stop.

Important things to remember

- I would suggest not picking a sport because you want to look a certain way. Pick a sport that makes you improve, you will stop caring about how you look and care more about how strong you are. If you are new to this, focus on how you feel, not how you are going to look.

- Never ever buy or read magazines. They thrive off self hate. They tell you how to be Hollywood Handsome and socially acceptable. Make no mistake, sports magazines are no better. You are training for you, not anybody else.

- Never compare yourself to anyone else. I once was floored by a tiny 5 foot korean girl who spent the whole session acting like a newbie. She nearly broke my wrist as she disarmed me.

- Competition is healthy but not being competitive is also okay. You don't need to be competitive to succeed in a gym, go at your pace, do your thing. No one will be thinking bad things of you and if they are, why do you care what they think? They probably have terrible eyebrows anyway. Your worth is not to be judged by the uninformed.

Starting a fitness adventure is the best choice you could ever make. Just make sure it's fun!

Also, I am sure you look fantastic in fitness wear. Go have some fun, you deserve it. You are awesome, fun, bright and fascinating.

MAINTENANCE

Yes. I did something borderline sexist and renamed self care to maintenance. It is also kind of insulting but also, most men aren't comfortable with the idea of self care. Self care has become a very feminine thing because the marketing companies have taken it over to sell eye creams and luxury products. Only women are allowed to have the luxury of self care but self care is important for you, you need to take care of yourself, it isn't anyone else's responsibility, no matter who you take care of.

I know you have been ignoring this so we are going to talk about your maintenance routine, as it is easily forgotten. People are busy, drained, tired, overworked, underpaid and overwhelmed. Let's be honest here, self care and men are rarely ever talked about. It should be but it isn't.

Which leads us to having zero energy to be lovin' thy body. You have to **HAVE TO** take care of yourself. This isn't a suggestion, this is a lifeline for you.

Self care doesn't mean bubble baths and shopping sprees, which is most of the problem. People associate self care with indulgent purchases and conventionally feminine activities. Even though most men I know love a shopping spree. I mean by all means, do that if you want to, but by self care, I mean doing the hard things too.

I love coffee but it makes me really socially anxious, caffeine does that and when I noticed that I was anxious on days I had coffee, I made the decision to quit coffee. I. **Love**. Coffee. This was hard but as a result, no anxiety. This is what I mean by self care.

It is taking time to cut out things from your life that are bad for you and making time for things that make you feel full in your soul.

You can't fight on the front lines if you are exhausted with a broken spirit. Race car drivers don't go out onto the track with an empty tank of gas, they stock up and then live their best life.

You need to refill your tank. It is much easier to focus on overcoming all these bad habits, toxic beliefs when you have the energy too and that's before you have to deal with the world. This world isn't built to make you feel good about yourself, there is no profit in that. If we all loved ourselves as we are, an unfathomable amount of businesses and industries would die. You hate your body because someone else is profiting off it. To fight that bad juju, you need a full tank of gas so let's talk about how you are going to take care of yourself.

Self care in relation to body acceptance

Let's talk pragmatics. What can you be doing everyday to work towards self care? Because success in anything is built on habits. Doing small things everyday to build towards a greater goal, the goal in this case being, your happiness.

Self care can be whatever makes you feel light and like yourself. If you haven't felt like that in a long time, that is a really good hint that you need to do some self care, have some time for yourself.

Think about things you did that made you feel light and happy. It can be a fun activity, a thing you used to do, a ritual you used to do but you just don't do anymore. That is a great place to start and work it into a routine. Don't be afraid to experiment with things as well, I am always discovering new ways to make myself happy, I just discovered poetry which I have never ever been interested in ever but now I love it. You never know what you won't like until you try it.

Here are some things you can consider putting into your routine or things you should consider making yourself a priority.

If you are totally lost, here are my suggestions:

1. Get in nature. Swim in the sea, walk in forests, feel the breeze on the mountain tops.
2. Exercise
3. Meditate or yoga
4. Video game or read
5. Grow something, grow a plant. Don't be sad if it dies, get a succulent.
6. Dance
7. Practice daily gratitude
8. Journal
9. Turn off social for a day
10. Mental Health Day
11. Binge netflix and chill
12. Sit with your feelings
13. Clean up your environment and Maria Kondo your life
14. Pet a dog or an animal
15. Go for an adventure

Make a routine that is ideal for you and actually do it.

Your routine will be unique, it doesn't have to be daily, it doesn't have to be hours long. It can be a few small things each day or one big thing each week. Just make time to reconnect with who you are.

It is important to know that not everyday is a good day, don't be so hard on yourself. Somedays are hard and you find yourself hating your body. In your self care routine, you have to have a bit of compassion and forgiveness. You aren't perfect and that is okay.

Let's dive into a few of these because they are important.

Get a plant

This sounds weirder than it is. Get a plant, give it a name and treat it well. Your body is the plant (remember earlier when I banged on about your inner voice being like a plant?). Treat your new pot plant like your baby, learn how to care for it and then do care for it. If you are worried that you kill all plants, fear not, get a succulent, germanium or a flaming katy. If you feel like you got this, get an orchid. Having something else to care for and keep alive helps you move that practice over to yourself. Also, plants give off all the good vibes, even if you are a plant murderer (hi *ghost Jade waves in shame*), get an aloe, it will never die.

Adventure

We talked about this already but workout from a place of fun and excitement and not from a place of trying to change your body. Instead of going to the gym to work out, go for a walk in a forest or skateboarding. Use exercise to take care of yourself and reconnect with your body, your body can do so much more than you think it can.

Letting go of perfection

You are not perfect and that is okay. An important part of self care is letting go of the idea that you have to be perfect and stop shaming yourself for the way you think you have failed. On your body acceptance journey, you are going to have days where you just relapse and think about all the ways you hate your body and then you are going to shame yourself for thinking like that. Like you should be perfect and flawless at loving yourself immediately.

When the leaves on trees turn yellow in the autumn and fall off, do you think they have failed? No, that is what they are supposed to do. You aren't supposed to bloom all year around because you aren't supposed to be perfect. You are perfectly imperfect and you need to cut yourself some slack, some days are just awful. Some days are just ballbustingly awful but the journey to body acceptance is supposed to be a rollercoaster of a ride. I said at the start it is like visiting a theme park. Well I hate to tell you but roller coasters are all over the place, not all rides are lazy rivers. Some throw you about and make you projectile vomit. But that doesn't mean you are a bad person if you throw up, it just means you're on the journey and the ride was a little too much for you at that moment (maybe you ate a hotdog pre-ride) and that is great. Leaves are supposed to grow yellow and die so that next season they can come back stronger. Let go of the idea of perfection, you are allowed to stumble, just make it part of your dance.

You aren't perfect and that is okay.

Emotional Cleansing

Now my beautiful rainbow, we need to talk about clearing out your feelings. There is a chapter called "Man Up" on this but here is the long and short of it. If you have a build up of feelings like overwhelm, anger, it will make healing that much harder. You need to focus on what you are feeling and why.

For example, I was once really angry and irritable for days and I was standing in the living room seething at some socks on the floor and it just suddenly hit me like a ton of bricks. I realised it was because I was feeling unappreciated for all the hard work that I did. I can't make people appreciate me (control what you can control) so I went out of my way to make myself feel appreciated and others. Suddenly my mood changed exponentially for the better because I was taking better care of myself and my emotional needs.

We talk about mental health a lot but no one ever talks about how you should identify what you are feeling and pragmatically come up with solutions to help you deal with them. If you are feeling insecure, why? What is it that would make you feel more secure? Do it for yourself or have a direct conversation. Take control of your feelings and deal with them.

Social Media

We will talk about beauty standards later on but your social media, especially if you spend a lot of time on it (want to know how much? Check your app). I am all for diversifying your feed. I love seeing all spectrums but if you are following people who make you feel like crap, hide and unfollow. This includes friends and people you know. You can just mute their posts if they are stressing you out. Follow pages that make you happy, help you feel inspired. We go to social media to relax so make sure your feed is relaxing and fun. Not just filled with unrealistic bodies and expectations.

We spend so much time on social media these days that are the perfect conditions to grow your belief plants. If you follow negative feeds that make you feel bad about your body, your I hate my body belief plant will grow bigger as Patrick continues to water it. Whereas if you clean up your feed and focus on the positive, it is so much easier to make sure you keep Velma and Patrick focused on watering the right belief plant.

Representation Matters

Representation matters whether you think it does or not. Your brain is complex and it is a lot smarter than you think it is. Your brain is constantly picking up subconscious information to feed into your beliefs about bodies. For example,

You will go online shopping, you see a nice t-shirt and you buy it.

It comes, it looks meh on you and you don't blame the shirt, you blame your body for not looking like the super tanned, white teeth jacked model on the website. And Patrick files that piece of information in the filing cabinet of 'I am not good enough unless I look like'. Regardless of the reality that maybe the t-shirt just wasn't that poppin'.

Representation isn't something you can control, you cannot companies and media outlets have a diverse range of body types. That is a change that will come around in time but for now, we need to talk about representation. You need to diversify your feeds and get in front and support businesses that use body diversity. Follow artists, models, influencers, businesses, friends, people who represent your body type. This is a form of self care. Right now, it is split in the media, we have a host of body positive activists (AMAZING!) and we have the traditional jacked bodies (also AMAZING! Remember, all bodies are beautiful, it's not any body's fault that theirs was chosen to be broadcast everywhere). But you, like many people, may have noticed that there isn't any mid-sized representation, age or colour diversity at all in mainstream media.

So go find it. Exposure to diverse body types will stop you feeling isolated in your body image. Like you are the only person in the world who doesn't look like that.

We know why this happens. (Good ol' Velma and Patrick). Your brain believes that you should look a certain way and your brain looks for reasons to back this up. You will ignore body diversity and only notice the ideal body type that you are not so it will feed into the belief of what you should look like. We need to make sure Velma and Patrick are getting exposed to the right kind of content.

Don't feel like this is just you by the way, this has been me my whole life. As we live more and more online the reality is you are seeing less and less normal bodies and seeing more and more photoshopped bodies. Your brain cannot tell the difference when you scroll past something in 2 seconds and your brain is smart. It will see the same body type and lots of views, likes comments and clicks and it will put two and two together that if you look like that, you will be successful and anyone else is just lucky. It is the incorrect conclusion but it happens. Like I said, Patrick is a sharp cookie and great at its job.

If you want to let go of these old beliefs, surround yourself with people who represent your body type, size, colour and age who make you feel empowered and happy. Change your algorithms, change the media outlets and shops you shop at.

Who are you hanging with?

You know that classic phrase, you are a combination of the 5 people you hang out with? Well, it is true. If you are hanging out with negative minded people who hate their bodies and spend all day talking about how much they hate their bodies and judging others, you will hate your body.

Here is an example:

You are with your friend Quillam, they point at someone (a person smaller and younger than you) and say "Oh my god, haven't they gotten fat". And you just nod thinking, "hey, that's a harmless comment right. It is technically accurate."

Wrong my friend, wrong. For too many reasons but you don't have all day. The main problem is that you instantly size yourself up against that person. Velma and Patrick are listening and they are meticulous. You compare, you think to yourself, "oh my god, me too" and the shame sinks in subconsciously as if good ol' Quilly's just insulted you to your face. It can hurt when people make critical comments about your and others bodies because it feels like every bad thought you've ever had about yourself is valid but it isn't. It's just an opinion and an opinion is subjective, it isn't a fact.

If you noticed that the other point was that their body is none of yours or Quilly's business then Great Job! Have a cupcake. *Ghost Jade hands you a cupcake*

You are absorbing hate through osmosis. Through pure association, you can't control what they want to say or do or think. But you can choose not to put yourself in those kinds of situations.

Now, you can call them out and explain to them what is happening and how it's hurting everyone, especially you. Personally, I love to respond with a positive compliment about their body. A lot of the negative rhetoric we say is automated, we don't think about it, we just parrot. By responding with a positive response, it can shock the person into realising what they are saying.

You should know that most body shaming comments are just other people projecting their insecurities or ideals of how things "should be" based on social conditioning and not how things actually are. Mostly due to constantly and relentless bullying from the media and marketing campaigns. But yet again, I digress, more on that later.

Hang out with people who make you feel happy, supported and wonderful. Expand your circle, make new friends or ask your current friends to go on this journey with you. I have always found when you decide you are worth a shit and start taking steps towards that, you will shed pounds of unwanted social associations.

You know one of my favourite phrases I heard is that "misery likes company". I heard it when I was 23 and sometimes I worked with someone who was trying to convince me to smoke with her on work breaks. When you decide not to partake in the smoking or miserable parade of hating oneself and others, they tend not to enjoy your company and they take themselves to their own parties.

Embrace change, you deserve a happy, body lovin' life and things will have to shift. Remember, it's not about you, you are awesome, some people just can't see past their own pain to be happy for you.

Environment

Transiting casually into the next area of self care, let's talk about your life. Where are you living? Working? What is your house like? Desk?

Your mindset is built up off your environment, if you live in a tip that doesn't bring you joy, you will feel like crap. Make sure every part of your life makes you smile. Get rid of that exes scarf that makes you sad (you aren't living in a Taylor Swift song), ditch those old pizza boxes. Maria Kondo your life. If you don't need it or it doesn't bring you happiness, donate it, sell it, throw it. Repaint your house if you have too. Change your background on your phone to something happy. Inspire yourself everyday without even having to think about it.

Now your activities for this section are easy and fun if you are a nerd like me *Ghost Jade throws a notepad at you*

Activity number 1. Maintenance plan

Write a list of all the things that make you feel great about you, things that are important to your self care and print it out. Make it easily accessible so that you can easily reference it for the days that you are paralytically stuck in your own head.

Make it pretty, easy to read and then make a weekly and daily routine that works for you and do it.

Activity number 2. Go as you mean to go on.

Clear up your life. Your environment, your social media, your inbox, your friends, your life. Go as you mean to go on.

Write down who you want to be, what you want to do and what kind of people you want in your life and start to make those changes. If you don't know where to start, clean one room and buy a pot plant. Feel the reward and then repeat, clean up and replace it with something that provides nothing but love.

Toxic Relationships

This is actually the perfect time to talk about something that is really hard to talk about. Toxic relationships. Letting go of toxic relationships is imperative to your self care and not just for your body, but your soul. We don't want to think our friends and family are toxic but we have to talk about it because you never know who in your life loves you but can't deal with you being happy.

Do you feel like you have one in your life? You justify them being in your life but you feel like if there was anyone stomping on your rose bush in your head when you aren't looking, it's them.

I think on some level, everyone can be toxic to someone. We can all be bad influences and bring people down without meaning to or intention. But does that make us bad people?

I don't think so. If you have a toxic person and you have realised it, they probably have no idea they are toxic because they are so wrapped up in their own mental health issues that they can't see the devastation they reep. But also, we all have mental health issues and sometimes we take them out on other people by accident.

But how do you know if a person is toxic or not?

When you hang out with them, do you leave you feeling drained, upset, defensive but you don't know why?

You no longer trust them because they have lied to you on more than one occasion about something small but the truth came out and they weren't apologetic for it. Or they say one thing and then say a completely opposite thing so there is no consistency to what they say.

You don't like yourself when you are with them. Like they turn you into someone you're not and make you discuss or do things that make you really uncomfortable

You **know** they talk shit about you. You just know it.

They are two faced, as the toxic person's closest person, they will compliment someone and then turn around and insult them for the same thing.

They compete with you about everything. Everything is a competition to beat you and they think they are better than you and try to assert that over you regularly.

You can't depend on their advice, if they listen to you at all. It's like you try and talk about your problems but they get shut down or change the subject to their own problems or something they want to discuss and most commonly, that is giving backhanded compliments. Like Oh yeah but you are looking really skinny, you know who's looking really fat? *insert a friend's name who is smaller than you*.

You are Embarrassed by their behaviour towards others. When they act a certain way or say things about other people and you are actually embarrassed by the terrible things they are saying.

And of course, you make excuses for them. If a toxic person has put you in a bad position and you keep making excuses for them, that is toxic.

They make you feel belittled and insecure and you feel like you are getting their problems as well as your own.

Toxic people are the hardest because it is not that they are bad people but they are being bad friends. We all go through rough patches and we all struggle but I am going to say something devastatingly blunt so be prepared.

It is not your responsibility to help your toxic person. It is their responsibility. More often than not, toxic people don't want to get better or improve because they think they are fine as they are and all the people turning away from them are the crazy ones. You are not responsible for their behaviour.

But once you realise you have a toxic person in your life, you are not only responsible for your actions moving forward but also the choice you have to make and it's not an easy one.

The choice is to walk away and protect yourself, your mental health and your body image.

If their behaviour is getting so bad it's bringing you down and making you hate yourself and your body, you have to put yourself first. You don't owe them anything. I know it may seem like you do but at the end of the day, you are your first priority.

Being a good person and being toxic are not the same thing.

You can be a good person and be a toxic influence on someone. Good people have mental health issues and toxic views on how bodies should be. Good people can be mean, intentionally or not. Not all toxic people are self obsessed narcissists, they come dressed in all shapes and sizes.

Meaning, the question then becomes, do you love yourself enough to become an adult? To step away from the drama and negativity you have been caught up in?

Are you brave enough to face your own insecurities about why you are still in this toxic relationship and challenge your own preconceptions of what you deserve?

Do you know what happens when you step away from toxic people?

All the good things.

Everything is nice and smooth. This has happened before to me but with a toxic person I was dating (more than once but I learn slowly), all these good things just started happening. I felt so much lighter without that negativity and drama in my life.

You aren't in control of their actions or their behaviours but you can put enough distance between yourself and them to give them the opportunity to develop and grow and for you to focus on yourself unhindered by the constant negative emotions that your toxic person is dragging you down and making you feel awful for your body shape.

If you do feel like you have a person in your life that is, shall we say, holding you back from your awesome loving self, you should walk away.

Cut contact with the person. Take space. Put yourself first. Don't make the mistake of thinking this can just be partners or friends. This can be family members too. Co-workers. They can be closer to you than you think. You just have to take a step back out of the whole situation and assess what is happening to you right now. Is it you? No? Then it is them? Find out and make the changes so you can both move forward away from the negative cycle.

What is the process?

Everyone is different but this is how it works for me. To start with, say you are taking some space. Take the space you need and don't message or interact with them unless you have to.

Writing your feelings can really help, writing a goodbye letter to them to help process and let go of the feelings you are going through.

I am a big believer in direct conversations. Once you have gotten your thoughts in order, sit and have a calm and collected conversation with how you have been feeling and explain how their actions are affecting you. Always take responsibility for your part in the dynamic, you aren't perfect, none of us are. In the ideal situation, your person will happily agree and you will both work to change and thrive. If your direct conversation doesn't go well and you leave feeling awful, it is time to load up the dump truck.

Being the dumper is the hardest part of a toxic breakup, you have to handle the guilt and responsibility, being dumped you get to say "Oh they didn't appreciate me for who I was" and they get to continue denying that they are the problem.

Set some limits. Have a limit on how much you are going to interact and stick to it, don't deviate. If you said you are cutting it down to 15 minute conversation a day instead of 2 hours. Do it. Hang up.

Normally I don't suggest this, this is if the person gets nasty because from experience, that can happen. Do the Ghost. *Ghost Jade does the ghost dance*

Start to reply slowly if at all, give it loads of time in between each conversation and just be polite but take as much space as they allow and hopefully, they will get bored and move on.

In the event that you call out on the fact that you are ghosting them, it is time to be more direct. Tell them you were really upset but what happened and you are taking your space and tell her the boundaries you have set.

Remember that often toxic people have no interest in hearing about your feelings or anything that isn't what they want, so keep it calm and neutral.

Don't rise to their bait. When they are attempting to goad you, say this is upsetting me, I am not going to talk to you while you are like this and stop replying. Even if 100 apology messages come through. Take at least 24 hours to recover emotionally from the altercation.

Now you have set the boundaries or told them your relationship was important to you but now it's time to move on, there will be 2 outcomes.

- They will happily go and be chill.

- They will fight using their most underhanded methods. Often using things like gang mentality or how you owe them.

Keep your emotions in check, stay calm and do not buy into their reactive behaviour. Stay firm in your decision and by this point, it means you can cut them out.

Breaking up with a toxic person is an endless plethora of feelings and emotions. One moment you are angry and then you see a photo or remember a good time and you are sad, you will go through the whole grieving process which is the hardest bit, you are suffering from a loss but you are in control of it. You will be angry, you will feel like a total idiot, you will feel guilty but also like you have been betrayed, manipulated and lied to. It is all part of the process of cutting ties with them.

Stepping out of the cycle you are in will also feel like a breath of fresh air, like you feel like yourself again.

You can do this, find people in your life who love you and focus solely on them. Your real people will come out of the woodwork and be there for you. This is the most helpful quote I have ever heard and when I was going through this, my friend gave this to me.

Those who mind, Don't Matter.

And those that matter, Don't Mind.

If I can give you any advice, it would be to reach out to your real friends you trust. See if you can find someone who has been through something similar, buy them tea and ask them about what happened to them.

Don't care about the haters, one day, they are going to be where you are right now and when they are, show them the compassion that they didn't show you.

How do you know you aren't the toxic one?

This is something I recently expanded upon but If you aren't sure, you have a few options:

Seek help, go to the therapist and explain what happened and what they are like and talk it out with them. An outsiders opinion will be a fantastic help to help you work out if it's your behaviour that is the problem or not.

Talk to your closest friends, the people who know and ask for some honest feedback and yes, it could hurt. Assure them that you aren't going to get aggressive and over react and ask them to be 100% honest with you. Hearing the truth hurts but they will tell you if you are toxic or not and if you are, you now know and you can work on these problems so they don't affect your future friendships. Take the feedback on board in a calm manner, your friends are trusting you to be calm and collected, don't get defensive, we all try hard to be our best and it is underappreciated a lot of the time and it can feel like a personal attack, but it isn't.

But if you are not, they will tell you and provide ample amounts of evidence as to why you aren't the crazy one, even if you feel like it. Your friends and family will be honest with you about your shortcomings, if they think you have any.

To be honest, if you want a shortcut, ask the person you are involved with as your best friend, and they will tell you straight.

You could be the toxic person causing all the drama or you could be the victim caught up in the landslide.

That got heavy for a bit, I know it seems really odd to include an entire segment on social relationships but if you are trying to break free of hating your body, one thing that will always hold you back is a toxic person in your life using your hatred of your body to control you. You don't need that, you deserve so much more. Like I said at the start of this book, this is a theme park, all the rides are different. Maybe this section wasn't for you but someone out there needed to hear it and if you did, you aren't alone and you are worthy.

This is what I meant by the way when I suggested you take this book one chapter at a time. Put the book down and do a deep clean, make a plan. You can read all you want but change is made through action. *Ghost Jade grabs the dustpan for you*.

Go make some changes and stop reading... Nerd.

Said the Queen of Nerds who is in 3 different book clubs. You look great today by the way! I love what you have done with your soul, it is looking luminous.

C O N F I D E N C E 101

If you want to feel confident in your body, you have to understand how confidence works. People often think confidence is something you are born with or given. It isn't. It is something you earn by putting yourself out there and smashing against the tide, over and over again.

I have not always been a confident person, in fact, I have been chronically shy most of my life. Confidence was not born to me, I had to earn it or more specifically, learn it. I was that kid in school who would never put their hand up, even if I knew the answer because I strongly dislike attention. It always baffled me how people are seemingly born so confident, even if they aren't like superheros.

The second I was old enough, society and the media stripped me of my confidence. I remember feeling alone, like everyone else confident and cheerful and me all alone, the chonky failure.

The years flew by and I learned that confidence isn't born, it is forged. Through people who were brave enough to get pushed down and get up again anyway and keep talking, keep pushing with no assurance that they would be well received. Confidence has never been a born gift, it is just a weapon of the fearless. Confident people are fearless and all I had to do was pick up a sword and shield and be brave.

Confidence Vs Arrogance

I want to address the fundamental difference between confidence and arrogance. It is often presumed that to be confident is to be arrogant. That simply isn't true. Confidence is trust in one's ability to do something and it is built through trial and error and experience. Arrogance is thinking you are better than somebody because you are more skilled than them. Confidence is an attribute, arrogance is an attitude and a bad one at that.

For example:
"I have an amazing body, it is hot and sexy" - Confidence
"I have an amazing body, it is hot and sexier than yours"- Rude for one thing but also arrogant
"I have an amazing body, it is hot and sexy and so do you" - Doing Ghost Jade proud

There is nothing wrong with being confident, it's actually necessary to progress in life, you have to take those steps forward and you will be confident in some areas of your life. You can sit and tell me you have no confidence but there is something in your life you feel confident doing. Like taking the bus, brushing your teeth, painting portraits of ghosts.

We are all confident, we just decided one day it was safer not to be confident because to gain confidence is to practice new skills and risk failure and abject humiliation and we would rather be safe than progress and that is why we are unhappy.

We aren't built to stagnante, it's not in our nature. We love adrenaline, new shiny and exciting, we aren't built to live on the safe side of life, that is why we are such a successful species, it's why we are exceptionally innovative. It's time to stop playing it safe and step up and accept that you are a confident person, you are just more confident in some areas than not. And for the areas you aren't strong at (like wearing budgie smugglers on the beach), doesn't mean you aren't confident at all, it just means in that area, you aren't confident.

The story you are telling yourself that you aren't confident is causing more harm than good.

Here is the secret formula to growing confidence.

Find what you're afraid of and do it. Over and Over again.

Are you afraid of what people will think of you if you do something?
Do it, see how it goes and realise no one really cares.

Afraid of wearing less than 10 layers on the beach?
Do it, see how it goes and inspire someone else to do the same.

Confidence is just you failing over and over at something until you aren't afraid anymore. Simple.

But in the event it isn't as simple as that, here are some helpful nuggets of wisdom to help you along your journey to confidence.

Nuggets of Confidence

Nugget 1- Don't Give

Don't give two shits about what anyone thinks of you. I'm being serious. Not your mother, not your partner, not the queen Bee. If you wanna dance in a fountain, you go ahead. If you want to dress like a t rex, you go ahead (you'd probably bump into me...in the fountain dressed as a t-rex).

Not everyone is going to like you, in fact, if someone doesn't not like you, you're doing something wrong.
Everytime someone throws away the idea that they should act a certain way to be accepted, the world becomes a more inspiring place. And sure, you're gonna offend somebody but you are going to inspire somebody and it's going to be awesome.

If you want to be confident, shed the lie that you have to be a certain way and you should care what people think of you. People will hate you for you and people will love you for you. The result is that you get to be you. Don't change who you are to keep somebody, they either accept you for who you are and who you want to be or they don't and it's their loss.

Nugget 2: Present yourself with confidence

Presentation is everything. If you present yourself with confidence, as I have mentioned many times before, your brain will find ways to reinforce the behaviour until it becomes a habit. Act with confidence and your brain will find ways for you to gain it.

Something you may feel is fraud syndrome, feeling like you are a fake. Breathe, you are just acting, like in a play. Don't lie, just be brave, be loud and don't be afraid to be wrong. It becomes easier, especially when it comes to your body. Remember, loving yourself isn't arrogant.

Nugget 3: Always accept a compliment

Need I discuss this more? Of course! This is so important. It is rude not to accept a compliment. If someone compliments you and you say, "oh no, this old thing or no you are mistaken". You are insulting their taste. Always say thank you, show gratitude that they went out of their way to find something they liked about you and told you. Say "thank you". Full Stop. Then you can cringe all you want.

With regards to fake compliments that are intended as backhanded or even insults, always say thank you anyway. Nothing is more annoying to someone trying to insult your body than you taking the compliment as it isn't intended. If someone says a rude compliment, you smile and say "Oh Thank You" and wink. The more sincerely you accept the unintended compliment, the more hilarious.

Next time someone compliments your body, just say thank you. You can blush like a firetruck if you want but say thanks. Because I can promise you that when you call them crazy for complimenting you, you could be hurting their feelings.

If you feel like reaching the next level, when you receive a compliment, follow it up with "thanks, I am also handsome and smart". If you are ballsy enough to drop that kind of confidence, you are unstoppable.

Nugget 4: See a problem as a challenge

Challenges are inevitable in life, to build confidence in ourselves, we are easily shaken by facing adversity and then going "Oh My God, it's too hard, I am weak and unworthy because I don't know how to face this problem".
Instead, I want you to look at the problem and shout, "I CAN DO DIFFICULT THINGS".

Visualise yourself headbutting throught the problem and say "This is just a challenge, I am great at overcoming challenges, here are 3 examples in my life where I overcame a difficult challenge. I can do this, I just need to find a way and I relish the opportunity to grow".

Nugget 5: Avoid criticising others

This is important to our own confidence because being critical spreads negativity. If someone needs some negative feedback like Person A is being a dick and needs to be told so (Quilliam for example), then that is okay. But don't criticise others for their interests and hobbies, don't criticise them for who they are and what they do. You just don't understand them and the less you criticise and start to empathise, the better emotional language you will develop and it will make all of your social interactions more positive.

Nugget 6: Smile and look people in the eyes.

This one is important and the most difficult one for me. I struggle with eye contact because I find the contact overwhelming as it involves looking into their soul and seeing them. But I always make an effort to make eye contact to make people know that I see them and that they are heard and appreciated. If nothing else, looking into people's eyes creates real connection and the more connections you make, the more confident you will be about making more.

Nugget 7: Body posture

Stand up straighter, walk with confidence. How you sit, walk and lead is important to confidence. Body language says everything about ourselves to ourselves. I don't want you to do all of these nuggets for anybody else to believe you are confident, we are doing them for yourself. When I am interested and focused in the office my back goes solid straight and my focus is exactly. Replicate that feeling of confidence by adjusting your body to do so. It sounds cheesy but hey, change is uncomfortable.

Nugget 8: Dress with Confidence

Don't wait until you "lose that weight" or hit that "body goal" to wear nice clothes and feel attractive. I know how easy it is to not bother dressing up nice or buying clothes that you want because "I can do all of that stuff when I look the way I want too". But do not wait until your body is perfect to dress up and feel attractive. You can do that no matter what your body looks like, it's about attitude, not about your body.

A good thing to do for this would be to follow some fashion influencers who represent your body type. This will encourage you to wear things you want to wear because it reinforces the truth that you can wear whatever you want to wear in any body shape.

When you wake up, everyday, get dressed. I know it's so easy to stay in sweatpants (they are so cosy) and shove a hat on but you have to start dressing to make yourself happy. It doesn't have to be a lot, you don't have to go full three piece suit everyday. All I am saying is, throw out all of your clothes that don't make you feel great. Go buy clothes that you feel cute and handsome in, in the body you have now, no waiting until your body is "perfect". Everyday, make your bed, put on the pants that make you feel awesome, wash your face and head out into the world. Some days are made for sweatpants and coffee stained XL t-shirts but most days are built to dress awesome and win.

This really is a powerful asset for self confidence. If you dress knowing you feel and look great, you have that confidence boost. Put on your outfit that makes you feel like a badass, that can be a power suit or a battered old band t-shirt. (My friend Terry wears nothing but old Red Hot Chilli Pepper T shirts and he feels amazing in them, he looks it too) Your power is your power. Align it with your life.

Nugget 9: Stand up for yourself

You are treated how you allow yourself to be treated. This one is deep and not the funnest nugget. It's not easy to stand up for yourself but you have to stand up for yourself, your continued allowance of letting someone walk all over you means you are allowing the bad behaviour to happen.

People will come for you. People are going to say rude and hurtful things that will make you doubt your power (and you are damn powerful). It is part of day to day male culture. We call it bantering and we know they don't mean to offend but sometimes, they can. We can't control that but you can respond. You can take away their power by not letting their projecting trauma get to you. Personally, I love to laugh at people who body shame me because they sound so stupid.

Reminder: Just because people insult your body, doesn't mean they are right. Like I said, it hurts because they are validating all those insecure voices in your head that are telling you that you aren't good enough. But it is just their opinion and it's not true.

This takes practice but you can have responses ready like laughing at them. You know the phrase kill them with kindness? Smile patronisingly and be polite or better yet, reply with "You want to run that past me again fucktruck?" (but you didn't hear that from me). We are all different, find what works for you.

Standing up for yourself is terrifying but it is also empowering and most of the time, bullies back down because they don't know how to handle throwing back. You start to push back, they fold. Take back control of your life and stand up for yourself. If someone is taking advantage of you at work and getting you to do all their work, say no, report them to your boss, create some waves. The waves of change and start taking back control of your life. Same with a bossy mother-in-law, push back, if they hate you so what, it's a mutual relationship, don't be afraid, if anything, you may gain some respect.

Ghost Jade is a total nark and she lives for it. Snitches don't get stitches. Snitches get cupcakes

Nugget 10: Give genuine compliments to someone each day

Why is giving someone a compliment gaining your confidence? Because you will receive a compliment in return at some point and I don't care what you say, it boosts confidence to know your hard work is being appreciated.

It was recently made aware to me that my brother has never complimented anyone because he doesn't know how and he believes compliments are rewards for good behaviour.

They are not, compliments are expressions of appreciation of someone's act or things of beauty or in general, positivity. To compliment someone, find something about them that you find pleasing, start with something physical like "I like your scarf" or "nice buns, which bakery did you get it from?" and then practice more emotional ones like "I love the way you make the room light up when you talk" or "I really like your energy".

Complimenting is easy, everyone offers value in some form, just find it and tell them about it. Remember you are more than just a body and so is everyone else.

Nugget 11: Accept your imperfections

Perfectionism. We talked about this but it's nice to bring it back up again because we live in a perfectionist world. We aren't perfect, never will be and stop letting it hold you back from practising confidence. You will never be perfect, so the pursuit of perfection is a waste of time because perfection is a fluid and unattainable construct created by people who just want people to be better. The best in the world at things know they aren't perfect because there is always more to learn and grow. Get over it and just try stuff.

You are allowed to just be yourself. You don't have to be perfect. Just be you. You are amazing just as you are.

Nugget 12: Own It

Ghost Jade favourite confidence nugget. Embrace what you love doing and own it, if you step up and own it, confidence follows suit. My sister has a great theory, fashion is fashionable and looks good because you Own It. You wear it and you feel amazing and you own it. No matter if you are wearing a traffic cone. If you love it, it looks amazing on you and everyone sees it.

OWN IT. Experiment. Because no matter if people don't get it, you will look fantastic because your soul will shine through and you will look epic.

Owning what you are ashamed of is where confidence is forged. Even if people hate it (especially if people hate it). Own it. If someone critiques you, slap back with "AND WHAT?! I LOVE IT".

For me, this was with my big butt (back when it wasn't hip and happening to have a big butt). I just walked around and was like "Yeah I have a big butt and it's awesome" and you know what, people respect you for it. If you like wearing certain clothes that people think you shouldn't wear because of your body, own it. If you do things with your body that people don't approve of, own it. It's your body. You. Do You.

I cannot express how applicable this is to all areas of your life. You are awesome, whatever you love. Own it. You will never sound stupid because there is someone else out in this world that thinks you are the coolest person ever for owning it. Find your tribe. You don't have to be loved by millions or the people right next to you, you can find your tribe anywhere (yay internet!).

Nugget 13: Not Ready

Stop believing you are not ready for something, no one has ever been ready for something. Not even people convinced they are. Embrace this knowledge and use it to your advantage and stop trying to protect yourself. You keep trying to avoid the pain of embarrassment and humiliation by not putting yourself out there at the risk of looking like an idiot. You will never achieve something unless you accept that progress means you have to take a blind step forward into the darkness and look like a pratt. But no one is there laughing at you and if they laugh, you laugh back but harder.

Nugget 14: Don't take things personally.

I don't take things personally if people don't like me because of three things.

1. Sometimes it isn't about you, you are not the centre of the universe.

Sometimes people have bad days and they take it out on you or they just had other things happen. But other people have stuff going on too, 90% of the time I have felt offended or snubbed, there has been a very logical reason and most of the time, it's because other people struggle too. Be kind and don't take things personally, people aren't perfect.

2. Sometimes it is about you.

Sometimes people are triggered in weird and wonderful ways. Sometimes people just dislike what you believe in and all of these are not on you. You can't control other people, you can't control how they feel. That would be crazy. You can only listen and adjust your behaviour in the future to be considerate to that person. That is the only thing you can control. You can't take something back, you can't change what happened, you can learn, apologise if needed and move forward.

3. It doesn't matter.

If I cared what every single person thought of me, I would curl up in a ball and cry... forever. Humans are judgemental and not everyone is going to like me, in fact, a lot of people don't but that doesn't matter. Because someone not liking me doesn't affect my self worth. I am good enough even if people don't like me. I know we have a biological need to be liked but our survival does not depend on it anymore. Since our tribes are so big now, we can't care what everyone thinks of us. We can only care what we think of us, lest you go insane. You don't have to appease anyone but yourself and find validation from within. I know social media has encouraged us to become addicted to social validation but you have to validate yourself, else you will endlessly try and find it in other people and it isn't other people's responsibility to validate you.

Here is an example of what to:

Gary walks up to Anne (She is fabulously curvy in a very trendy pink corduroy oversized suit) and tells her that what she is wearing is doing nothing to hide the fact that she is fat and ugly.

She's offended, of course she is, someone just walked up to her face, judged her and was very rude to her face. Gary was lucky he didn't receive a knuckle sandwich.

But why did he say that? What provoked him to verbally attack Anne like that?

Let's take a look at Gary, he is going through a bitter divorce and he has put on some weight. He is a man of structure, like things to conform to the social norms and putting on weight is something he is struggling with. He woke up feeling incredibly alone in the world, looking down into the chasm that is depression and looking forward all he sees is darkness, confusion and disorder.

Do you feel differently about how Gary commented now?
Maybe a little, some empathy started kicking in now that you've got some perspective but it is still unbelievably rude but this is the reality we live in, people project their problems.

Now comes what Anne should do. Everyone has bad days and these interactions happen, sometimes on a daily basis. How do you handle them?

I'll tell you what Anne did, she was momentarily offended (fist curling knuckle sandwich dispensing time), then remembered this most powerful statement.

It was not about me.

This lesson is golden, it extends to whenever anyone is lashing out at you because they are angry and unappreciated. When your parent or boss is having a bad day and she shouts at you because they picked something, just remember it is not about you.

Take a deep breath to control your anger and shock, think, it was not about me and contemplate how they are feeling, what led them to that outburst. Here is when you should probably ask "are you alright?". Most of the time you'll get a rude remark or get snapped at but if you scratch the surface, you'll see the person underneath just trying to hold it together.

Do this and you'll be free. Free from being angry at passive and/or aggressive people all the time, from personal criticism because it doesn't matter what anyone thinks of you, they should love you for you. If they don't, find someone that will, even then, not everyone has to love you. Get comfortable with people not liking you, you will be so much happier.

The same goes for people that do not agree with you, many people won't. There is a huge need for everyone to agree on one thing and if you do not agree, you are chastised. Try not to be that guy who tells you you're wrong because you believe in something different. Politely disagree, listen to their points and know that if they don't want to listen to yours, that is fine, just don't waste time with them when you could be eating ice cream in Portugal.

You are confident. YOU ARE. You are just confident in different places but I am confident in you. Confidence is just another plant to grow in your garden. You have to tell Velma to plant the seed and make sure Patrick gets all the information he needs to help that plant thrive.

You are awesome. You are exceptional. You can do anything you set your handsome mind to. You have unlimited potential. You hear me? Limitless potential. I can't for you to take your power and rise to greatness because you can and because you deserve to. You are worthy.

You can be confident, it just takes practice and overcoming fears on the daily.

Feel the Fear and Do It Anyway.

A book you need to read by Susan Jeffers.

GRATITUDE

This chapter is small because it's a simple concept, this is more of a reminder for you really and the next chapter is heavy so embrace the short chapter while it lasts.

I always start with this but I want you to treat your body as if it was a child, your child. Some of you may be younger so think of your body as someone you love. It is important because when you love and want to protect someone, you don't think about their shortcomings, unless they have spilled pasta sauce all over your sofa. You see them for their beautiful selves. Once you shatter the illusion of beauty, you see people not for how they aren't good enough but for all that they are and the world brightens.

This is where the power of gratitude comes in. Gratitude is the superpower that makes the world a better place. We live for more, better, stronger, newer, cooler, now, it is just the instant society we live in. When I was young warthog, we would listen to albums thousands of times (cause CDs were expensive) *Ghost Jade waves her walking stick*. These days, I listen to an album 4 times and I am over it, I want something new and better. With this attitude it is easy to forget all we have as we search for more.

Gratitude brings us back from a mindset of lack and not good enough to abundance and fulfilment. It is an amazing tool to help you disconnect this idea that your self worth is connected to your body shape.

We are most ungrateful to our bodies as we relentlessly punish them for never being good enough. Vexed that they aren't everything we dream they are going to be so we can get to the places we want to go. My bad body image has held me back from doing way too many things I want to do in my life, not my body. I never did something because I was like, "I can't do that, if I lost weight and I was skinny, I could then do this". "I can't possibly wear this bikini, travel, start a blog, apply to be a model, apply for a promotion, ask that person out".

Never giving myself permission to do things I wanted to do because I was afraid of being judged by my body. Shame. It wasn't my body's fault, I could still do these things, I was the problem.

Anyway, we're talking about gratitude.

You are ungrateful for your body because it doesn't look the way that society wants.

It doesn't look the way that you want it. You think that if you have the right body shape, you can do the stuff that you've always wanted to do.

You have thoughts like:
"Why is my body so annoying?"
"It's so frustrating"
"Why is it I so much as look at a snack and gain 10 pounds"
"I'm so angry because it isn't the shape I need it to be so I can do the things that I want to do"
"If I just looked like him, I would be fine"
"I want to go travelling but I can't because I'm not in shape"
"I want to play rugby but I am too small"
"I want to ask out that girl but I am too short and she is taller than me"
"I want to do this pole dancing class but I can't because I'm not in the right shape"
"I want to ask this guy out but I am too skinny, he will never like me"

Nothing is stopping you doing those things that you can do regardless of the shape of your body. There is nothing stopping you doing the things that you want to do.

But this obsession with being ungrateful and frustrated with your body has to stop because it is destroying not only your self-esteem but your relationship with your body.

It's time to reconnect and be grateful for your body because there are so many things to be grateful for.

Your body is amazing. Do one biology class and you will see how cool if you get cut, your skin stitches itself back together.

It grows new cells in your body.

It's incredible the way that you see stuff, the way that you hear, the way that you smell like a really nice cinnamon bun

Your body is so incredible.
It grows fingernails.
It protects you automatically if you're falling over. Your brain does this to protect you, to protect your face.

Your body can reach, stretch and dance.
It can move.
It can do such amazing, wonderful things.
It heals.

Your body is absolutely fascinating.

Your body is a tool to experience life with. It is not an ornament to impress people with.

What we want to do is instead of focusing on all that it's not, we want to focus on all that it is. Focus on all the wonderful things that it does.

For example, I am grateful right now for the fact that I don't have any ulcers in my face.

You know what this is like? Potholes on the roads.

We're always annoyed that there's a pothole but we're never grateful that it's not there.
We're like "There's a pothole. How annoying, I have to avoid it, I fall into it, I hate potholes"
Then "oh, they've closed the road to fix the pothole, how annoying. I will be late for work".

And then when it's gone, we're not grateful that it isn't there. We focus on the annoyance and negativity but we never take a moment to appreciate how smooth the drive is when the pothole has been fixed.

It's the exact same thing with your body.

We need to practice gratitude for your wonderful, amazing body. I am grateful for so many things about my body, even if it's not the ideal shape, even if it is not the way that I've always wanted it to be.

I am happier in a bigger size than I was when I was small, because when I was obsessed with being the "perfect shape" and the "perfect size", I was always miserable and I was always at war with my body and I was always ungrateful.

Now that I'm in this space where I love my body and it's bigger and I'm just so happy and I'm so full of abundance and light, my life is so much more exciting and interesting and adventurous because I'm doing stuff regardless of the shape of my body.

I'm not wasting so much time obsessing about shrinking and starving it into a shape the society would appreciate. Or working out and obsessing over muscle gain so much it takes up my entire day and thinking power.

But you know what? No matter what shape or size you are, society never appreciates it. You'll never get the appreciation you're looking for by changing the shape of your body.

No matter how much I start, no matter how much weight I've ever lost, it's never enough.

Instead, I want to focus on how grateful you are to your body, there are so many reasons to be grateful.

You get to wake up.

You get to walk around, not everyone does.

You get to eat delicious foods.

You get to do all the fun things you want to do, watch tv, ride a bike, go to the zoo with ease.

Your body keeps you healthy, alive, functioning, healing without complaint. All it ever asks is that you feed and water it and we hate it for it.

Activity: Gratitude Daily

Everyday, I want you to think of something you are grateful for about your body.

Write it down, say it outloud, say it to someone, post it on social media. Whatever your process is, thank your body for its service.

There is something about your body that you like.

Start there and work your way up to the more difficult things.

By practising it every single day, you will take your head space from a place of hatred and negativity to a place of abundance. It will help fuel your new belief that your body is worthy and good enough. Gratitude is a great way to reinforce a new belief, it is a great way to keep Velma and Patrick watering your new belief plant that your body is amazing and beautiful.

Everyday for 30 days. Start with the easy bits, the parts you like and then as you grow and focus on disconnecting self worth with your body and society's depiction of beauty, you can focus on the harder parts to love. Jiggly thighs, injuries, diseases, cellulite, extra large pores. All those things society has told you to hate, eventually, through gratitude, you will learn to love them because you will love yourself as you are.

I am grateful for my eyes, my half a toe that reminds me of my sister and how amazing livers are, they regrow.

I am also grateful for you, you are amazing. I am grateful you are totally going to be grateful and I am mostly grateful that you are taking a risk and a chance to change and live your best life. It is worth it. I promise you. You are a breathtaking marvel.

"M A N U P"

In the original book I wrote for all genders, I didn't actually include this topic. This topic is going into the next book called Happiness. The reason I included it in this book is because to be honest, you put a lot of faith in me reading this one. This might be the only opportunity I get to give you this information so I am going to give it to you.

Also, you get to be a guinea pig which is nice. A fluffy one with tufts of hair in all directions.

This section is called Man Up but not in the way you think. Toxic masculinity has barred you from having or expressing feelings. Whenever you do, you get shamed or mocked or put down. Which sucks and I am sorry.

But hey, you still feel stuff so together, we are going to go through the tools you need to process your feelings and move forward, on the downlow.

It isn't specifically relevant to put in this book because it is more of a mindset issue than a body issue but that being said, I think the attitude of the Man Up way of life is the reason you are struggling with body issues.

You are told by literally everyone that you shouldn't have feelings, you should suck it up, suffer in silence.

But I want to bring something up.

Robin Williams, you remember him right? Actor, Icon, Epic Human. I do. Did you know he used to always put other people's happiness first because he knew what it was to be depressed and he didn't want that for anyone? He was a caring loving human and he committed suicide.

It was a sad day.

And we all say, all day long, "oh my gosh, why don't men speak out more" but the reality is, the world chats a lot of shit and does nothing to back it up.

Yeah, I said it.

The most horrific thing about Mr Williams is that if you knew, you would go and give him a hug and do everything you could to help him through his struggle because he offers so much value to the world. *Ghost Jade "well I would anyway"*

But you are a Robin Williams. You offer so much value to the world and you couldn't be a more exceptional human being.

But by denying your basic needs for emotional support and processing, you are putting yourself in a dangerous position.

Don't get me wrong, I am all for keeping my personal life and feelings to myself, I relate to the struggles you go with. I am not an oversharer. Showing emotional vulnerability is scary and I am not telling you to do anything. But don't feel the pressure to pretend you aren't feeling how you are feeling. How you feel is real and valid and repressing it and ignoring it is counter productive. The more you don't face your feelings and deal with them, the more pressure will build up and you will blow. You might blow up at someone, you might try and escape the pressure with a little something something, you might be driven to darker thoughts.

Instead of pretending you don't feel things, learn how to deal with your feelings. This next chapter is all about helping you deal and process your feelings. Do not let toxic masculinity convince you that you don't have feelings.

So, just between you and I, we are going to talk about how to process your feelings and you can do this and still have a masculine facade of manliness. You are still a man, you just have better mental health.

Emotional Balancing

Now, this is a practical exercise to help you get through your feelings your way. *Ghost Jade is a pragmatist* As I mentioned, I always refused to express my emotions so I found that journalling was best for me but some people love to talk it out with people, so do that. You do you. The wonders of this life is that you get to discover who you are and what works for you. I am going to give you the rundown of the system and you can test different ways to use it until you find a system that works for you.

Let's go over the basics.

There are 6 main emotions that are holding you back from happiness.

Fear, Guilt, Shame, Loss, Denial, Connection

We are also going to talk about anger but that is for later on. What this process does is actually make you face the emotion, validate it so you can move on. This process is really freeing, I know when I am struggling my imagination can run wild is an understatement. We sit and torture ourselves with the What Ifs, Everyone Hates Me, This Could Happen even though none of it is even true and won't actually happen. But we have no way to combat this wild imagination because no one ever taught us how, we more often than not, just wait it out until we are forced to face what is causing the problem.

This is an activity based exercise and there are so many different ways you can do this. Everyone is a different emotional processing machine so here are some ideas on ways you can do the exercise.

1. Write it down, get a notepad and write out the process.

2. Think through the process. Just put this article down and think your way through it, it is a form of meditation.

3. Think your way through it via exercise. Go on a walk and go through the process with each emotion.

4. Talk it out with someone, sit someone down and go through the process and ask them to prompt you for deeper answers.

This process is broken down into a very simple structure.

You work out why you are really struggling, the real reason, the raw unfiltered petty, sadistic, honest reason. Don't be afraid of who you are, you aren't perfect.

Reassurance. You reassure yourself that you are safe and that what you are feeling will not kill you.

Corrective language. You correct the narrative in your head from negative to reassuring and positive.

Just so you know, this emotional balancing isn't balanced. They cover emotions that we need to address and let go of but you may find that while you feel a lot of loss, you don't feel a lot of guilt. Which means you can spend ages working through all your fears, but 2 minutes working on your guilt because you are guilt free. This process is fluid like your emotions so roll with it and see how you feel. Always start with Fear as that is the one we struggle with most and work your way up the chain, if you feel comfortable with one, say a reassuring line them move on

For example, if you don't feel ashamed of anything, just say "I am proud of who I am and my life" and move straight on to Loss. I know that I have rushed past a few because I know that I am really struggling with one particular thing but it is always good to clear all of these emotional blocks.

Let's get started.

Grab a notepad, find a cosy spot to just chill out where you feel safe and secure. Take a deep breath and don't be afraid of who you are, you are just a person and that is okay.

FEAR

This is the most common one because we feel fear on a daily basis.

We can make this a visual.

Firstly, picture Ghost Jade at your side, armed with a bat, looking intimidating because she is the fierce protector of you. She loves you and she knows you can win.

Second, picture Fear. We shall call fear Flynn. However you see Flynn is how you see it.

We fear for our survival but in modern day, we aren't scared of tigers anymore. We are scared of answering the phone or what Brad from the office thinks of our hair because he is Queen Bee and if you aren't in with him, You Aren't Alive. We fear the loss of our social status, our house, what other people think of us. We are all just scared. All the time. It isn't our fault, the media uses our fear based mentality (our survival instinct) against us every day, no wonder we are all afraid. *Flynn is sat there posting fear mongering articles laughing maniacally*

So the first one we need to face is fear and it needs to be faced a lot because most of the time (and this is key) it won't kill you.

Let's start with putting it in perspective.

Grab a notepad and I want you to start a list of all the things you are scared of. I don't mean things like Bees and WW3. I mean the things you are emotionally scared of. Scared of losing someone, scared of being judged or shouted at. I want you to make a massive list of the things you fear and then one by one write down how they aren't going to kill you. All the things Flynn has been whispering to you when you aren't looking and Ghost Jade was distracted by a rather ampliy filled donut.

Once they are out there and you know they won't kill you, you can begin to face them and let them go. We often forget how much we have been through in our lives that we often feel beat down and defeated. But we are the ones who have defeated so much. Don't let fear stop you doing anything. Feel the fear and do it anyway and you will realise just how unscary it actually is.

How many times in your life has Flynn gone "No you can't do that, you will fail, everyone will hate you, you are a loser" But you did it anyway and showed them? Too many to count.

To summarise:

Identify what you are afraid of. Find what Flynn whispers to you.

Why are you afraid of it? I mean really why, none of this "I don't know" or vague guesses.

I want the deep meaningful "BECAUSE I AM AFRAID I WILL DIE ALONE AN OLD HAG BECAUSE NO ONE WILL EVER LOVE ME BECAUSE I AM TOO FAT" - Me dealing with my eating disorder 2014

Write down how it is not going to kill you and how it is absurd. Point out to Flynn that their whole fear mongering article is actually unsubstantiated claims based on hearsay and you are no longer amenable to this nonsense.

Then face it. Send that scary message. Do that scary activity. Face your fear knowing that you will still live to see another day.

For example:

I believe: "I am afraid of eating half a slice of cheesecake"

Flynn says "If you eat that, you will be fat"

Digging deeper It is because it will make me "put on weight" and I will be fat forever and no one will ever love me or find me attractive.

This cheesecake won't kill me and if someone doesn't like me for how I look, it is their loss. People will love me for what I look like and if they don't I have myself and I will love myself while I find someone else who will appreciate my body.

Eat the cheesecake, go on a dating site in a bikini and say "THIS IS ME FOLKS, LIKE IT OR NOT", I Am Awesome.

GUILT

We all feel guilty from time to time. It is actually more common than you think.

We feel guilty for being indulgent, spending time on ourselves instead of others so we just don't. We feel guilty for eating. For being ourselves. We feel guilty for the things we love (we all have a tv show that is our guilty pleasure #BorderControl). We feel guilty for betraying people even if it isn't intended. We feel guilty for things we did as stupid teenagers.

Guilt is the killer of pleasure.

When it comes to your guilty pleasures, it is time for you to take them out of the shame hut. Own it. Trust me. I did this, I took my shame TV Show and I went public and went I LIKE THIS SHOW and the world went What? ... *10 seconds past* .. Meh Whatever. No need to be ashamed because no one really cares and you will be amazed how many people you inspire to be themselves just by being real about who you are.

Guilt is always shaming you for your interests because you think people will judge you poorly for them. Grettel is a tricky mister, they sneak into your subconscious and shame you for things that to be honest, you have no reason to be ashamed about.

Let's talk about those guilty feelings from past transgressions. We all know the kind. Grab your notepad because we are about to process through your guilt so you can enjoy your life again

Write down all the things you feel guilty about. What is Grettel currently banginig on about and reminding you of a time.

1. Accept that these things have happened. You can't change it, what has happened has happened. All you can do is learn from it and move forwards.

2. Forgive yourself. Take a deep breath and go "I forgive my past self, I do the best I can with what I have and now I know better and will do better in the future".

3. Say I love myself for being myself.

Process through each thing. Look at the guilt, you can't change it, you can just move forward and learn from it. Make a physical symbol that you are forgiving yourself, drawing a line under the guilt and moving forward, maybe write it down, say it, dance the letters out. Whatever your process. You do you.

For example

Grettle reminds me that I feel guilty for letting my friend down by not being there for her when she needed me.

Point: I wasn't there, I couldn't have known, I did the best I could even though I wish I could have done more.

Forgive: I forgive myself for not being there for her and in future, I try to be there for her more.

Move on: I love myself.

SHAME

We touched on this in the last one but Let's Chat About Shame. We all feel ashamed about stuff, I mentioned our secret shameful guilty pleasures but shame can go much deeper than that. What are your biggest disappointments in yourself? What Are You Ashamed of?

Sawyer is a snakey one, slips shame into everyday life when you don't even need to be ashamed. It is easy really, it only takes a joke or an off comment and Sawyer appears with their snakey features and sinks their fangs in.

Grab the notepad, let me show you how to repel snakes.

Write down all the things you are ashamed of cause we are about to cross them off the list. What has Sawyer recently reminded you of?

Accept that these things you are ashamed of are a part of your life. They are who you are and you like them and there is nothing wrong with that, maybe some people won't accept them but if it brings you joy, it brings You Joy. Your joy is more important than their approval.

Your past transgression that you are ashamed of, they are in the past. Like guilt, you have to move forward, you can't change what happened. All you can do is apologise if needed and move forward. Forgive yourself for your past, you are doing better now. Your mistakes have helped make you Who You Are. Which means, your mistakes that you are ashamed of are a part of you. They kept creating you, moving you and building you into the person you are because you learned from them. You aren't perfect, let it go.

Own it. Just own it. Your mistakes, your choices, your interests. Be who you are and if it ruffles a feather then it ruffles a feather. But you get to be yourself and you being happy is more important than a few disgruntled people. Don't be ashamed of who you are, take responsibility for who you are, you aren't meant to be perfect, you aren't meant to be somebody else. You are meant to be You. *Ghost Jade rocks out the Rainbow flag*

For example

Sawyer prods me about my job.

Point: I am ashamed that I don't have a high paying job at my age.

Deal: If I got a high paying corporate job, I wouldn't have been able to travel as freely as I have. I wouldn't have been able to do the things I have done and I wouldn't have the friends I have. I may not have a high paying corporate job but the work I do is meaningful and it has given me the life I wanted. I do not conform to societal norms that I should have a job, get married and live happily ever after. I want something different and that doesn't mean my life is any less of value.

Move on: I am proud of my life, my choices and the good I bring to this world.

Suck it Sawyer.

LOSS

This is the hard one, we have all lost so much in our lives. Friendships, people, identities, pets, favourite shoes, iPhones. We lose a lot of things that mean stuff to us and it gets hard after a while.

I don't need to explain to you what you have lost because you have already visualised what it was that is still hurting so we are going to dive right in and meet Leona.

Leona, like all feelings are natural, when they come knocking, it is painful and loss is one of the most difficult emotions to process so no matter what. You do you, take your time, do what feels right.

Grab the notepad.

What have you lost in your life that still causes you grief? Write it down.

So for me, I have always found peace in this:

The love for your loss hasn't gone, it is still within you and although it may be gone, the love you had was real and it doesn't go away. It is like energy and it is reborn in the form of a new love. That love can be found in a new friend, partner, identity, community, animal or even a new pair of shoes (I am very attached to shoes).

For example

Point: I lost my cat 5 years ago and I still feel that loss in my soul.

Deal: But that love was real and although I don't get to see him physically, my love for him is found in my new cats, in the way to express love for him and the way I imagine he would knock things off the counter.

Move forward: Love is the cure to all so when we feel like we have lost something we love, it hurts. But love is energy and it always comes back to those who are willing to open their hearts up and look for a new love.

Now I know, once scorned no one wants to dip their toes back into the pit to be ripped apart again by a ravenous hound. Don't be afraid to open yourself up to love and try again, just be a lot more careful with whom you allow into your zone and don't be afraid, because even if that love goes, there will always be more because you are worthy of love and you love yourself.

That love you have lost, it is still there and it will always be. You are worthy of love, never forget that.

DENIAL

aka Your Own Bullshit.

Desmond is a funny old' one, it is great at distracting you. Denial, the lies we tell ourselves to make us feel better about ourselves. Need I Say More? We all like to tell ourselves lies to hide who we really are, underneath. Underneath all of the people telling us who we should be and what we should do, we deny parts of ourselves.

A huge part of this is the stories we tell ourselves, like I am not blah blah or I can't do this because of Blah Blah. We tell ourselves we can't do something and deny ourselves the opportunity to even try because We Told Ourselves We Can't.

Desmond loves to start the narrative that you can't or you aren't enough. But you need to accept who you are.

You need to accept that those stories you have been telling yourself aren't actual facts, they are just limiting beliefs.

You are Who You Are and you need to actually start expressing it. If you need some inspiration, check out the Entire LGBTQ+ community, they are who they are and they stopped denying it. How amazing. Don't deny this part of your life, if you are lying to yourself about your own nature, challenge it and own it.

Grab the damn notepad and let's remove Desmond from the building.

What stories are you telling yourself? What part of your life are you denying? What part of your soul are you denying because you are worried what people will think of it?

What are you hiding deep down in that psyche of yours?

Face each one, is it true? or is this something you could learn and work on?

Is this a solid part of your life? Do you feel bad about not expressing it?

Express yourself. I mean right now, announce to the world (aka yourself) that you are going to stop denying this part of your life.

For example:

Desmond: I can't sing

Fact: I can sing, just not very well, in fact it's pretty awful.

Deal: But, singing is a skill that can be learned so all I have to do is learn it and not being able to sing bums me out so I am going to learn to sing because I want to. I am no longer going to tell myself I can't, only that I am getting better!

Ghost Jade sings My Chemical Romance really R e a l l y loudly

Move on: Be true to who you are, don't hide it. Life is more interesting when you let yourself out.

CONNECTION

I want to talk about connection aka Colette, who loves to isolate you. Our lives are made around the connections we make with other people. Our connection to animals, the earth, the sea, our co-workers, our connections with our favourite shoes because they took us on really fun adventures.

A key to unhappiness is feeling disconnected. When one of these emotions are prevalent and someone makes you feel afraid, guilty, ashamed of who you are, you feel disconnected and you choose to disconnect to protect yourself. Colette likes to do that, it's just their thing, they like to remind you that you are alone in the world.

Another loss of connection is the connection to who you are. When you go through a lot of loss, especially of identities and ideals, you lose that connection to who you are and you feel despondent, lost and alone because you don't even have yourself to hang out with.

Grab the notepad, let's talk about reconnecting with yourself.

What are your core values? Who are you? You are a collection of your values, beliefs and experiences. So let's start with what you do believe in and what your values are. Are you living in alignment with them?

Reach out to people you love and trust, people who like you for you. No space for shitty friends here. If someone makes you feel disconnected from other people, reach out for support and your true friends will have your back. Slowly you will learn that their shitty opinions of you won't matter anyway and you can move on.

Isolation is a key factor in depression. If you feel alone and you feel disconnected from yourself, depression and struggle will follow.

Reconnect with who you are. Reconnect with people you love. Don't make this harder on yourself.

We live to find connections.

And that is the end of the process. I always end a session with the overwhelming knowledge that nothing really matters. Life is fleeting and the universe is ever expanding so there is no time to be ashamed or guilty. There is only learning, moving forwards and doing the best you can. Some of the more spiritual minded people may have noticed that this is really similar to a chakra cleansing, that was the inspiration for this but I have a one foot in the door feeling towards spirituality, I love it but I like to translate it so people who aren't interested in the spiritual community can still benefit from the lessons its teaches.

Now let's talk about the emotions we have that we pretend we don't have, but we do, anger.

ANGER

I decided to pick Agnes because I imagine Agnes would shout "Get off my lawn", pick the tennis balls off her walking aid and throw them at those rowdy kids.

Anger has always been a difficult emotion.

When it starts, it often seems unstoppable—as if we are never going to feel calm again. But it is also one of the emotions we are most often shamed for feeling.

Anger can be damaging when we allow it to fire us up so that we say the things we know will hurt the person who has provoked us, but that we do not necessarily believe. The person on the receiving end doesn't know that, however, so all they feel is our seemingly vindictive hate toward them.

This kind of unchecked anger and its wreckage can be irreparable. Daggers spat out in anger can chip away at our self-esteem, causing us to second guess ourselves at every corner.

Each of us experiences anger differently. Some people are easily angered and quick to react, some are simmering pots that build up into a boil, and others slowly let off steam as it shows up.
However we experience anger, we need to know that it is nothing to be ashamed of.
It is an emotion, one that we all have.

I'll say it again: there is no shame in anger. The distinction is that shame comes when we weaponize anger and use it to hurt other people. It is okay to be angry, it is not okay to be cruel.

I want to help you deal with your anger in a healthy way so that you cause as little devastation to your life as possible.

First there are a few things you should know about Anger.

Anger, like all emotions, comes in and out like the tide.
Huge crashing waves of anger come, causing devastation. In their wake is an eerily calm silence as it sinks back into the sea.

Anger is sadness' bodyguard

Behind every feeling of anger, is another feeling: sadness, loss, pain, regret, hurt, embarrassment, fear, shame, grief, overwhelm...you name it. Anger is like Ghost Jade who loses her shit because someone has violated your boundaries and she goes to town with an inflatable hammer.
To avoid feeling these feelings, we get angry as the ultimate protection. It is important to know that while we are angry, we are actually sad or whatever other precise emotion. Focusing on the underlying feeling is helpful because it helps us to regain and feel in control.

Hurt

It is easier to be angry at someone than it is to tell someone you are hurt.
Being hurt hurts. It is much easier to be angry and shout at others than it is to be vulnerable. Sometimes we aren't given that space to explain, and that means we need some space to let the situation diffuse so we can come back from a place of vulnerability and calmness.

Shouting often gets us nowhere

Getting angry doesn't actually get us the things we want. Often, as soon as the energy rises and the shouting begins, people stop listening. Anger makes fools of us all by making us a little deaf. If we are in a heated argument, each party feels attacked and both feel the need to defend. So we dig our heels in and refuse to show compassion.

Seven stages

It's helpful to understand the seven stages of anger. There are seven stages to being angry and upon reading them, I am sure you can relate. It works a lot like the grieving process in the way that we move through the system until we reach acceptance.

1. Rage: Pure blinding uncontrolled rage.
2. Retaliation: You want to hurt them like they hurt you.
3. Resentment: You resent them for hurting you.
4. Resignation: It has happened now—there is nothing you can do about it.
5. Realism: Perspective, you realise that it wasn't the earth-shattering debacle you thought it was.
6. Resolution: You find a way to come to terms with how you have been hurt and you begin to move on.
7. Release: You let go of those angry feelings toward someone.

Finally, compassion is the opposite of anger.

Practising empathy and seeing how the other person is feeling helps us to not feel so attacked. It gives us the ability to understand that we aren't the only ones hurt in a situation. Other people are hurting too, and by practising compassion, we calm our anger and reach a solution.

Now that we know a little about anger, how do we make sure that we handle it in a mindful and aware way?

There are a few things that we can do when we are angry:

Walk away

If you feel the anger rising into your mouth and about to burst out of your face, leave the situation, conversation, or location. Get away from who or whatever is triggering you to be angry and find a safe place to breathe and calm down.

Calm down

Once you are safe, there are lots of things you can do to help yourself calm down. Normally meditation or workouts are the most common suggestions, but that never worked for me. If I am angry, I have no interest in working out.

The Process
"Work out" what the feeling underneath your anger is. Who hides behind Agnes? Is it sadness? Is it a hit to your pride? Loss? Pain? Embarrassment? Shame? Find out what your anger is defending.

Feel that feeling

Feel your sadness, shame, loss, or pain, and breathe through it. Cry, express it, face it in whatever way you find yourself drawn to.

Own your anger

You were angry, own it. Don't blame it on other people, take responsibility. It is your job to calm yourself down, to fix what has been broken. No one is going to fix it for you anymore. Our parents used to put out our anger, but now we are responsible for controlling and managing it on our own.

Journal it out

Everyone processes anger uniquely, but instead of saying all the things you want to say to a person, say it to the journal. Pen it out. Every rage-filled statement. Let it flow out of your head and into a safe space. Then do it again and again until you feel calmer.

Chat it out to a friend

Once you feel calmer, chat to a trusted buddy about it and receive advice that comes from a good place of love.

Find a solution that is within your control

It's that simple. Remember to make it about you.

Face your problem when you are calm

Write a little presentation with all the points you want to cover and explain why this hurt your feelings and how you can avoid this situation in the future. Then present it in a calm and orderly fashion so the person receiving it can actually hear you and has the chance to grow too.

Practice forgiveness and know that grudges aren't healthy

Don't get me wrong, some people aren't worth forgiving. But we forgive other people for ourselves, not because they deserve it. Forgive but learn and don't fall into that trap again.

Take care of yourself a little more

If you are struggling and anger is defending you, it means you are struggling with sadness, loss, or any number of feelings. Take time to take care of yourself. Forcing yourself to move forward doesn't help anything. It'll only cause more problems down the line.

Think about what this experience has taught you

Specifically, think about what it has taught you about yourself. Did you uncover a new feeling or trigger or pattern of response?

Did you discover that you are in an unhealthy relationship with someone?
For every time you are angry, learn something new about yourself and your life.

Anger Issues

Remember, that all of these techniques are useful but if you are struggling with anger issues, there are always professionals out there for you. I don't even vaguely claim to be an anger management professional. I am just a Ghost, talking to a dude, about feelings.

Here is the secret that no one ever seems to mention.

It is more efficient to sit and feel sadness and your feelings than it is to deny it.

Denying it only drags it out and causes anxiety and stress. If you are sad, you are allowed to feel sad, in fact it's vital. You cannot have the sun without the moon. Sadness is one of those feelings that just needs to be heard, once you listen and feel your sadness, there is a moment where you peak and the pain drifts away and you feel relief. Feel your sadness, you will be less likely drawn into anger.

I hope that was helpful, that is my secret process to processing my feelings when they feel overwhelming. No need to involve other people, just you and Ghost Jade.

Who thinks you are amazing, smart, cool, collected and you have a great taste in shirts.

F O O D

Trigger Warning: Disordered Eating. Skip to the next chapter if you need to.

You know, when I first wrote this, I was terrified and I still am and with that in mind, I want to start with a basic disclaimer. I am not a nutrition coach, I am not trained in that field. I cannot advise you on what is the best way to eat. I am going to give you some facts that helped me on my journey to self acceptance that revolve around food.

That being said, I want to give you all the information that helped me come to terms with food and body. It can be distressing and if you want to skip this chapter, please do. It might not even be relevant to you, if you have a great relationship with food, good for you! Move on with your day to the next section.

Remember, this is a theme park, you are more than welcome to disagree with what I say. Everything in this book is stuff that helped me heal, helped me love my body. Now let's get into it. Food.

As someone who has had body dysmorphia, binge eating disorder, anorexia, exorexia and orthorexia before, this is hard to talk about. Food and I have always been at war and all I can say is, there are books, coaches and doctors who are offering help. Go find it. Don't think you need this disease to survive or be loved, you are loved without it. I used to think that you never really recover from ED but as time moves forward, I feel healed.

I want to start with one SOLID Fact.

Food has no moral value

Food isn't good or bad. It just is.

Food can be nutritious and non nutritious. By assigning it good and bad means that it has a moral value and by consuming it you are good or bad.

You are not good or bad because of the food you eat. You just are, Whether you eat rather nutritiously or in the middle or not at all. The choice is yours.

This is a really hard topic to comprehend because we live in a society that says fat is "unhealthy" but actually, that's not true.

Fat isn't bad. It isn't unhealthy. I know a lot of products and brands try to convince you that it is but just because you have fat on your body, doesn't mean you are unhealthy. I know a lot of curvier men who are stronger, faster and fitter than me. Fat isn't unhealthy, that is the fact you need to remove from your head. Healthiness is not measured by how your body looks.

I know a lot of people who are bigger than me, have more fat on their body than me that are much healthier, much fitter and much stronger. Just never underestimate someone's body shape and size. Sometimes a person's body isn't a reflection of their lifestyle.

Never underestimate someone's body shape as a way of discerning whether they're a good or bad person. We need to stop saying and thinking things like "They must eat unhealthy foods, therefore they're a bad person". You have to stop doing that kind of crap because it's not helping you. It's not helping anyone and it's not even true.

That's the biggest lie of all. The society has taught us to say that just because someone has a bigger body that they are unhealthy and someone in a smaller body is healthy.
When that is not true at all, you can be healthy in any shape, body, any at all, small or big.

Let us dive into the most important nuggets of knowledge that helped me.

Nugget 1: Death To Diet Culture

Diet Culture. My eternal nemesis.

First up, don't get me wrong, if you want to lose weight, good for you! You do you! If you want to stay at your weight and love your body, GOOD FOR YOU! If you want to gain weight, GOOD FOR YOU! As a love of bodybuilding and fitness, I understand wanting to shred or bulk. I don't care what you do with your body, my issue is with Diet Culture. That who hath tortured us for our whole lives. Your body is your choice, I just want you to let go of the idea that your body isn't good enough because it is.

That is because my handsome human, everything you know about weight loss and bodies has been taught to you by marketing. As long as you hate your body, someone is profiting on it. (Yeah even me right now, hypocritical right? But the difference is, I want you to be happy, they want you to hate yourself more).

My issue isn't with weight loss. It's with the idea that you have to look a certain way to have value. That's what diet culture shoves down our throats on a daily basis.

Now like me, you probably have spent your WHOLE life being made to feel like your body isn't good enough and as a result, you need to change it in order to... what?

Be loved? Be attractive? Successful? Win at life? It's personal to each of us but here we are, trying to achieve the ideal body so finally society will accept us and we can not feel anxiety about what we eat and just enjoy life.

But like toxic abusive ex partners, you will never be good enough for society. Not even when they come back around, claiming they have changed with their fake body positive articles. Not even if you look like perfection, there will always be more, better.

Diet culture is so ingrained in our society that we see it everywhere, it dominates social conversations and products and goals. This was my first stage, understanding that actually, I didn't need to diet to be worth a damn. I could love myself and be happy, regardless of my body shape. My body shape didn't affect my success levels or my relationship status, everything was still good. Better even because when I let go of diet culture, I actually accelerated in happiness and growth although I will say, this was the last thing to go. It takes time to stab diet culture in the heart and rip it out. Patience is a virtue but by all means, if you want to tell it to fork off immediately, please do! Make me proud.

Nugget 2: How Weight Loss Actually Works: Science Style. No Bullshit Diets

Now before we even get into this, I want to say one thing loud and clear. I don't think you need to lose weight. I think your body is beautiful as it is. The purpose of this topic is to explain to you with science how weight loss works so you can ditch all the bullshit diets and just eat like a human. That does not mean that you should feel bad about wanting to lose weight. (I have to repeat myself and I will because I know how you think, I think it too). It is your life. If you want to lose weight, you are welcome too, there is no judgement either way. In fact, later on I am going to dive into weight loss and a body acceptance mindset if that is something you are interested in. Remember, this is a theme park, not a to do list, not every ride is meant just for you.

Define: Eat like a human

Y'all eat whatever it is you damn well want.

I am not here to tell you what to do because as I have said, it is your life.

The reason I want to get into it is because all my life, I have been plagued with not knowing how weight loss really works and therefore being so much more susceptible to new fad diets, pills and laxative teas. Information is power and I want to give you all the information you need to understand how weight loss works so you can know that No Matter what a weight loss program or product says it can do for you, it can't or it always comes back to the calorie deficit. Companies have been overcomplicating weight loss for years and amplifying your insecurity about your body to sell you more bullshit. Don't buy it. For example, Weight Loss Tea. A weight loss tea doesn't actually work, it just makes you poop more. Now, if you do enjoy shitting multiple times a day because you feel fresh, you can get the same result with a high fibre diet. *Ghost Jade is holding up a box of Bran Flakes and dried figs*

No matter what, these products don't work and I want to get into eating like a human but first, let's get into the nitty gritty of science.

Throw out everything you know about weight loss right now. Just take it outta your head and toss it in the trash. It is all utter garbage. It is just professionals trying to confuse you to sell their products or weight loss plans that are stupid, unsustainable and built in picking your insecurity apart. They have to create new ones because you tried one of their crappy diets and it didn't work so they rebranded it, switched it up. Every crappy article you have read in a magazine saying Ketones make you lose weight faster, keto diets, Atkins diet, how insulin affects your body causes weight loss issues. Unless you actually have a medical condition or you are trying to get that last 10% of body fat off, weight loss is simple.

Weight loss is just maths and consistency.

Introducing The Calorie Deficit.

Imagine you get paid your salary from work each month, let's say £1000.

If you spend over £1000 a month, you go into debt.

If you save some money cause you are a good little saver, you go into credit and you have some savings.

If you spend EXACTLY £1000 in the month, you will be exactly where you are right now.

This is weight loss.

Everyday you get your salary of calories and every day, you either go into debt, go into credit, or just even out.

If you keep overspending, you get further and further into debt aka Fat.

If you keep saving, you get a nice juicy bank balance to blow on a nice holiday to France aka weight loss.

If you live at your maintenance, which is the amount of food you need to function, you stay the same.

That is all, that is it. You wanna lose weight, it literally is, eat less and move more. Now I say all this because I want you to know how weight loss works so it stops being so damn confusing because weight loss is confusing. You will be bombarded with weight loss pills, magic potions and tactics and no matter what, you need to know that it is all bullshirt and the only way to lose weight is a calorie deficit.

Please note, this has been heavy on weight loss but this also applies to weight gain. You want to gain weight, consume more calories. That is the theory and the logic. I can't say it applies to all bodies, just a vast amount of them.

And now I want to get onto the topic of why you shouldn't focus your life on losing weight because your body wants to survive

Oh and just so you know, just because in the example, fat is described as debt, doesn't make it bad. I know you thought it because I thought it too. We don't think like that anymore. CAN IT Clarence. *Ghost Jade flips off Clarence*

Nugget 3: Why Weight Loss Is Hard and The Power of Intuitive Eating

This is where it gets complicated because a calorie deficit is complicit with diet culture and unless you need to lose weight for medical reasons, you don't have to. We are going to chat about intuitive eating and of course, your natural body. Your body isn't supposed to lose weight, scientifically, your body's job is to gain weight.

Your body has something called a set point. Which is the ideal weight your body decided is ideal for you to survive and thrive. Society may not deem it beautiful but regardless, it is beautiful because your body is beautiful no matter what size it is at. *Ghost Jade: "You wait until we get into the beauty standards chapter, the sass gets heavy".*

Let me introduce you to a book called Health At Every Size and to summarise a very challenging book for you as best I can. Your body isn't built to lose weight. Some are but they are a minority. Bodies are built to retain fat, for survival. Which means, to lose weight, goes against biology and you aren't just fighting delicious snacks. You are fighting against your biological programming. Your body fights you at every corner. It makes high fat foods smell more amazing, it slows your metabolism, it will allow you to lose a little weight but then it will fight you tooth and nail to keep your fat on your body. You are not the problem, the odds are stacked against you biologically speaking.

The problem isn't weight loss, sometimes weight loss is good. But your body has a set point that it has decided is healthy for you. Everyones is different. At some point, your body just goes, this is the weight you should be and sticks there.

I will explain this through my personal experience.
I sit at a solid 65kg. If I put on weight, it is really easy for me to lose weight up until this point. If I try to lose below 65kg, my body fights me the whole way. It wants me to be this size. It shed unnecessary weight but when it hits this point, it sticks. Everyone's set point is different which means all our bodies are designed to be different and wonderful shapes. HOW GREAT IS THAT! There is no one standard of beauty that is decided by mother nature. She made us all unique and powerful and that is a wonderful thing.

You are supposed to be the size you are. You aren't supposed to be anything other than what you are. If you are skinny, you just are. If you have fat on your body, you just are. You are supposed to be like that. That can either bring you peace or it will traumatise you because you have to live with the idea that you may never look like the way you have been telling yourself you should like all these years. Next section we are actually going to talk about the grieving process of dealing with this because it is hard. Knowing that you may never look like the way you think you should, losing that is a loss and it's okay. I have been there. But also, you are supposed to look the way you look and the way you look is goddamn handsome.

Nugget 4: We are biologically programmed to find pleasure in food.

Om Forking Nom.

The human animal is built to survive, survival means eating food to put on survival fat, (fat is good for survival) our brain is a smart cookie and finds ways for us to avoid starvation and find the highest calorie food available and encourages us to like it so we eat it more.

Now, I believe fat is good. How much fat someone has does not determine if someone is healthy or not. There are many size zero crack addicts that aren't healthy but in the eyes of society they are. I know many curvy men and women who are strong, fit and healthy but in the eyes of society, they aren't healthy at all. Our body shapes and the size of them isn't a testament to how healthy we are.

But now that calorie dense food is available everywhere, that biological programming still works and we are naturally drawn to sugar and fats. High in calories, energy and deliciousness. Biologically, this would mean berries and nuts. But, this food is making us put on our survival fat and since this isn't the caveman days and society believes fat and imperfection is evil, we began something called Restriction.

Aka. **Die**ts.

Restriction is a huge component to why Food FOMO is real. Human beings are rebels. If you tell us we can't do something, you can be damn sure that is what we are going to do. So when you say, you can't have that, "it's bad for you". Your brain doesn't hear the "it's bad for you", it hears the "You Can't" and then goes into a blind rage to get you that one item with its sneaky underhanded tactics.

Here is an example:

Restriction Mindset

I have Ben and Jerry's, I started eating it, it is delicious. Then I hit a point where I am done but my brain in restricted mode goes, "but Jade, you will never get this opportunity to eat this again, this is your one shot to enjoy this, get in as much as you can". As a result, I eat more than I intended to and shame myself.

126

Non Restriction Mindset

I have Ben and Jerry's, I started eating it, it is very delicious. I hit the point where I am done, I put it back in the freezer. Because I know, if I want some later, tomorrow, next year, I can have it. Hell I could eat the whole tub, I just don't want to.

This is because our body experiences dieting or restriction as a stressor. When we're stressed, we produce high-levels of cortisol and adrenaline (stress hormones). All our body is trying to do is keep us alive and as healthy as it can, every day, all day long and as a result, it responds poorly to restriction.

Your body will also enhance the pleasure receptors in your brain when you smell forbidden fruits, making them more appealing and weakening your willpower. Not only are foods more appealing to you when you say you can't have them, you can't enjoy them as much because of all the shaming and it makes you binge unnecessarily.

Which brings us to Bingeing.

Diets don't work because in this totally scientific way, we are rebels (as previously mentioned). We love what we are told we can't have, it's why we're such a successful species. We break the barriers of what is possible because we crave and challenge the impossible. Just take a moment, think of a time in your life where you were told that something you wanted was wrong and it was all you wanted.

Here are some classic examples

- Desserts
- Bad partners
- Stuff you can't afford

Diets don't work because they suck and they aren't sustainable. You can start on a diet with will power but then willpower doesn't last forever unless you are very committed.

Diets don't work because our brains have defence mechanisms to deal with starvation or diets. If you starve yourself too much, you enter binge mode where your brain compels you to consume as much as you can with no off switch because you need calories. Your body doesn't know when it's getting calories again so it binges to stock up for the impending starvation that is to follow.

Food affects us in many ways including mental health but the first thing you need to do is stop shaming yourself for the food you eat. It's important.

Nugget 5: Eating Like A Human

The intuitive eating way of living is my favourite lesson that I learnt. Basically, listen to your body and eat accordingly. No Shame. No Drama. Letting go of the idea of how I should eat and just listening to your body is fascinating. You have to ditch it all, eating at set times, eating set meals. If I want a bag of crisps for dinner and a pile of steamed veggies in hoisin sauce for breakfast, then so be it. Your body KNOWS what it wants and needs, it even craves things that have nutrients that it knows you need.

Sometimes you just have to let go of the idea that you know how to eat and just follow your natural cravings. I am all for eating healthy because I find processed foods make me feel down but I know so many people who don't have that. We are ALL different, which means this journey is totally unique to you. I wish I could offer a full on roadmap but I can't, this is an experiment, trial and error and experience.

Nugget 6: Why Eating Nutritious Is Important Nugget

Now, I don't eat healthy to lose weight because diets ruin everything. They ruin the basic joy that is eating delicious food but I do choose to eat healthy because it is good for your mental health.

I talk about this a lot but I believe in eating healthy foods for your Mental Health. Not for weight loss or weight management, pure and simply, to help you be happy and keep on top of your mental health.

Crazy I know? I know because if I eat healthy and wholesome food that makes me feel good, I feel indestructible, beautiful and powerful. I also have more energy, easier to think positive and my skin is radiant. When you eat healthy, you glow.

What do I mean by healthy eating?

Eating food is such a complex subject and it is filled with emotional triggers. I know it is filled with trauma so I hope to explain this in a chill and scientific way.

By healthy eating I mean eating food that makes you feel good and that is good for you. Filled with nutrients, fats, protein and vitamins. We all know what I mean because we all think we should eat more of it. I am chatting about wholesome food and veggies, non processed food that was made in a factory. Cooking from scratch. That sort of thing.

Let's talk about Science. The ideal human diet that is perfect for us to thrive mentally.

I want to start with the basics, the ideal human diet is a grain, nut, seed and legume diet. Yes guys, I am talking about plants! (Yaaay plants!) That is the "Ideal". A vegetarian diet filled with vegetables, legumes and nuts is what we are designed to eat. This is from a biological standpoint. It is ideal for growing healthy cells and helping you live a longer and happier life. The fun thing about eating a wholesome diet is that it doesn't take long to adjust, when you experience the benefits of feeling lighter, healthier and happier, saying no to processed food becomes easier. I come from a family of meat munchers myself so if you are a meat muncher, as long as you eat free range, you won't hear a peep outta me. You do you! I hear bacon is the bees knees.

How is healthy eating biological good for your mental health?

Let's chat about Gut Microbiology with my Top Fun Facts!

1. The gut has a mind of its own, around the same cells as a brain does, they are both interconnected. When we say we make decisions based on our stomachs, it's scientifically backed. (For reals)

2. 90% of the serotonin created in your body is created in your gut. So your happiness hormone is primarily created in your stomach.

To cut a long story short, your brain health is dependent on the quality of food you put into your gut because the microbes in there control everything. If you treat your stomach like a trash can, filling it with crappy foods with loads of chemicals, sugar and hormones. You Will Think Like Shit.

There is an amazing ted talk on this if you are interested. Food for thought: How your belly controls your brain by Ruairi Robertson.

Instant Gratification vs Delayed Gratification

Alright I hear you, but snacks guys! Does that mean I can't have them ever again? Of course not! It is your life. Your choice and I would never say don't eat a delicious snack, I love M&Ms.

Instant gratification- Instant (or immediate) gratification is a term that refers to the temptation, and resulting tendency, to forgo a future benefit in order to obtain a less rewarding but more immediate benefit (these are our snackos).

Delayed gratification- Delay of gratification, the act of resisting an impulse to take an immediately available reward in the hope of obtaining a more-valued reward in the future (saying no to the snackos for future mental health).

This is the eternal battle with sugar, having to say no to instant gratification to ensure a healthier future for yourself. This becomes a whole lot easier when you let go of the idea of restriction. We are biologically programmed to look and crave high fat and sugar foods, and the food industry knows this and uses it to sell you processed products. These products are not good for you which is why delayed gratification is important, questioning the impulse and saying no is good for healthy eating. What you eat today affects your mental health tomorrow. That is how I see it. That doesn't stop me having a pizza night because I know I can always come back to healthy eating and feel better and I can enjoy myself much more when I have the pizza. It is all about balance and yes that is super annoying because it's obvious, patronisingly so.

How to work out what food is nutritious and what isn't for you

Having to work out what triggers and causes my eczema, I have an abundance of practice in eating foods and listening to how my body feels after. I know that cheddar cheese, the most delicious food ever, doesn't agree with my skin, neither does aspartame and bread. Hilariously, I get rashes in different places for each one.

This is purely a 'go by how you feel' thing. People have different bodies and digestive systems which means, it is different for everyone which means... experimentation time!

If you need a guidebook, try Michael Pollan's food rules. It is a little outdated but this was my starting point, it gave me an idea of what to eat and what to not eat. The most important thing to do is enjoy the food you eat. If you are eating boring, bleh healthy food, it is never worth it. Make sure when you eat nutritiously, it is spectacular.

How often should I be eating nutritiously? All the time?

Noo. Not all the time, again the choice is up to you. If you find you feel better eating cleaner, eat it more. If you want more snackos, eat more snackos. I am not here to tell you how to eat, I am here to hopefully convince you that eating healthy is good for your overall mental health and brains!

Benefits of eating nutritiously

- Better Skin. Glow from the inside out.
- Reduced risk of diseases
- Improved gut health which leads to overall better mental health
- More energy
- Better sleep
- Compliments. People will be like "Oh My You Are So Healthy" and you get to go, Yah It's The Best Way. #SmugRights
- There are many more! But I think if these don't sway you, then I don't think I will be able to!

Finally, need some Inspo? Here is what I do!

- Open all your cookbooks and get marking pages.
- Get on BBC good food and google by category of meal.
- Ask 10 of your friends for their top recipes.
- Play Take Away Recreations. They taste so much better than the originals.

- Follow 3 blogs and watch their posts each week.
- The Bosh Cookbooks are Phenomenal. You can even add meat to all of them if that's your thing.

I love eating healthy because I love being happy. Eating healthy makes me happy. Biologically thanks to all the serotonin and emotionally thanks to a rich and fulfilling diet of strawberries.

Jades Eating Theory

Oh lord I know, this has been an info dump for the ages so here is my working theory that seems to work for me.

Once again, I have to remind you that you know you. You know YOUR life, what works for you works for you. This is just what worked for me.

I've lived the fad diets, the 8 hour walks a day on 500 calories of shit food. The crippling fear of food had meant that all I lived off was sweets, diet cola and multiple triple caramel frappuccinos.

But do you know what the worst part is? The confusion.

What is good for you? What is it to eat healthy?

And then you get told, some stuff you thought was good for you is bad. And things you thought were bad are actually good but really they are so bad for you they give you cancer.

I remember being 16 and being told that actually the yellow part of the egg is the better part and not the fatty part so we should all eat yolks now. It's just an Egg.

The worst part of it all is, when you think you got a handle on, when you think you Know. You go on social media and some other nutritionist, coach, doctor, person has the opposite opinion of it and you doubt yourself.

The good news is, I can simplify it for you and it's not a diet, it's not restrictive and no it's not a fad movement. Delete the word Diet from your brain.

To eat healthy and feel better, improve your skin, mood and serotonin levels you just have to follow these simple rules.
1. Eat more plants and vegetables, be plant positive. 80% of the time 20% snacks.
2. Eat the rainbow, not just beige.
3. Learn to cook, make it a passion of yours.
4. Drink water. Buckets of it. (But not too much and make sure you keep your electrolytes in).
5. Reduce the amount of processed food but don't restrict, you want something, have it.
6. Celebrate what you eat.
7. Always cook double so you can have leftovers for days when you are too tired to cook.

It is that simple.

Cook more, eat more natural foods but don't restrict yourself. If you fancy a takeaway pizza, then have one. Why not? I am a massive Ben and Jerry's netflix and chill fan.

And that massive long chapter is everything I have EVER learnt about food and helped me heal my relationship with it. Remember there are so many resources out there, you can heal from a disordered relationship with food. You don't need it. Reach out and find someone and let it go.

You are beautiful by the way, in case you forgot to tell yourself today.

Alright, go make a cup of tea and breathe. You are beautiful by the way and you look fantastic and your body is beautiful and you know what? That is the least interesting thing about you.

Part Three:

It's a Wild World

BODY SHAMING

Welcome to Part 3: It's a Wild World.

Firstly, if you think I wasn't annoyed that I couldn't find any male body diverse line art images available, you would be wrong. This is 90% off the problem with the body positive and body acceptance movement. Men are seemingly forgotten and it really chaps my ass to be honest. I can't change the world for you but I can let you know that the world isn't against you and you deserve love and acceptance as much as the next human.

The entire point of this section is to help you get to a point in your life where you can walk down the street and not feel insecure about your body. Not feel like everyone is staring at you and judging you for how you look because they aren't. But that all starts with us, by changing our attitudes on how we perceive ourselves and bodies in general, we can completely change the way we see the world.

Before we even dive into this area, here is my fundamental truth for you. This fact, this key phrase helps me deal with social anxiety, insecurities and everything in between.

Control what you can control.

You cannot control people, their hate, their thoughts, their choices. You can't control them, you can only control yourself.

When someone thinks a negative thought about you? You can't control that.

You can only control how you respond to it.

You can choose to pay attention, take their opinion as fact and hate yourself. Or you can choose to say no, actually, that is just your opinion. I am worthy regardless of that.

You cannot control every asshat in this world, you can only control you.

I am laying this into you because it can change how you take on the world. We spend our whole lives desperately trying to control other people, through pleasing people and persuasion. But when you let go of the idea of needing people to like you, approve of you, you are free.

It is not about not respecting other people's opinions, it is about knowing that no matter what anyone says, you are worth a damn and your body's worth is not up for debate. With anyone. Ever.

Now that we know we can't control them, let's talk about them.

Body shamers. We have all met one, that is why we have the issues we have. It is why you are here because someone shamed you into hating your body. It could have been a family member, friend, bully, magazine article, off comment by someone in the street.

We can't control that, those comments have happened and we can't change that. They handed Velma the seeds to plant so that the self hate bush could grow but that is the past, we are focused on the now and the future.

We cannot control what other people say or think, that isn't what this is about. When I say body shamers, I am not talking about other people, I am talking about **you**.

You are the biggest body shamer you know. You are the one who shames your body, every damn day. This needs to stop, no excuses. None at all. No "but I need it to make me disciplined or grow or be better". It has never bought you joy, don't lie to yourself anymore. It is time to let go of the internal body shaming. *Ghost Jade give you the sassiest look*

This isn't easy, I have bad days and it is okay. Some days I look in the mirror and go, "I love you body but also think, man my belly".

It all starts with taking on board these lessons and using corrective behaviour. When we hear those words forming in our brain, we hear them and then we say NO because our new life motto is.

We do not shame anymore.

You need to find your key phrase, for me, one of my key phrases is "We don't do that here" and "we don't think like that anymore". These are my powerful little key phrases to have in the back of your mind.

Now when I think, "you are not good enough, no one will love you if you don't look like *insert generic person I am comparing myself too*". Ghost Jade pops up, slaps and goes: "NO! We don't do that here".

And then we reassure ourselves that:

I am not perfect and that is okay.

I am still attractive because of who I am and also, my body is awesome just because it doesn't appeal to society's level of beauty doesn't mean it isn't beautiful.

I can't control if someone doesn't like my body and to be honest, it is none of their business.

My body is exceptional and it's mine, nobody else's. *Ghost Jade: "and so is yours"*

Bare with this analogy cause it's nuttier than a nut butter store.

We have these negative thoughts but they are like bats trapped in a belfry. Picture a dark belfry, it's cold and all the windows are boarded up and occasionally you open the hatch and throw in a bat (aka negative judgements about your body) to live there and they sit in the belfry, dormant. Until one day, something knocks the bell and all the bats go haywire, flying around, knocking into each other. It's overwhelming and chaotic and you can't do anything but think about how you aren't good enough. There is nowhere for the bats to leave either, they just keep flapping until they get tired or until you're mentally and emotionally drained and you curl up in bed praying tomorrow is better.

You have to stop criticising yourself for what you look like, it starts with catching those tired old phrases that you have learnt, battering around your belfry. Open the windows, let the bats out.

It does get easier. The harder you fight back, the easier the war becomes. You don't have to do this alone, that is why you reach out to your friends and you create an imaginary ghost friend called Jade who is there to remind you. I mean you can rename the Ghost friend sure, I always liked the name Crackers. Because you have to be crackers to love yourself in a world that is desperately trying to convince you otherwise. But here is the long held secret of us happy people. There is no such thing as normal and we are all crackers.

Embrace who you are no matter what. Not everyone will understand but that isn't their job. Your job is to be you and find your people, your tribe, you insane group of humans who get you.

Body Preconceptions

I want to talk about our shameful preconceptions about our bodies. How it affects our daily lives, relationships and is underhandedly, ruining our lives.

Growing up, I always dreamed of being skinny, like when I was a kid. Because to me, to be skinny is to:
- Be happy
- Be popular
- Have no problems

- Not be criticised or bullied
- To have an easy life
- To get everything you want
- To be accepted no matter what
- Easy, you can eat anything you want

For you guys, it may be the Chad body type (the nickname for the 6 pack stacked tanned Hollywood movie star) or whatever body type you find to be the ideal.

I want to talk about the first time this preconception about male beauty was challenged. Meet my now friend, Osric. Perfect doesn't quite cut it, Osric was the personification of beauty, 8% body fat, flawless skin, perfect floofy hair, abs for day, tall (although everyone is tall to little old me) and chiselled. He looked like a model. When I first met him I made those judgements that you make. "Dear lord, he is pretty, he must hate me for not being pretty. I bet he was born with a perfect body type, I bet he is really vain and selfish. He clearly doesn't like me because I am a chunkysarus. I bet everything is handed to him. I bet he can eat anything that he wants".

They are built into us, these weird and rude preconceptions about people. In the original book, I talk about it from a female perspective but Osric was another time my perception of beauty was challenged greatly because you have these weird beliefs about body types. It took me a while to warm up to Osric because these preconceptions made me so nervous and to be honest, super judgemental. I didn't hate him but my negativity towards him wasn't outwardly apparent but it was still there, buried under the surface. Affecting every interaction with him and keeping myself distant because he made me feel insecure and unworthy because my body wasn't "perfect" and therefore incompatible with his life.

After a while, I warmed up to him and then I learned something that blew my mind. Osric may be handsome looking but he is a solidly great guy. Kind, open minded, funny, sure his family owned a boat but hey, no one is perfect. He also struggled a lot with body issues, even though he looked like Hercules.

And The Thing That Really Blew Me Away.

Osric wasn't immune to body issues, no matter how perfect you perceive someone to be, everyone has body issues.

My preconceptions stopped me from making a real friend because of my assumptions about his body. Body shaming goes both ways.

Long story short, we are BFFs now.

Skinny or fat, old or young, male, female or androgynous, no matter what your body looks like, you are always going to be bullied or shamed. Life is always going to be hard and no matter what, being accepted and popular is a choice. It is all a choice. You can choose who you hang out with, you choose to listen to someone body shaming you or not, you choose what you eat, you choose to have problems because of something else you do.

All of the things I thought changing my body could solve, they couldn't. The only thing that could give me those things I wanted was to change my attitude. To create a life where I felt accepted by myself, have friends who made me feel wanted, eat whatever I wanted and say no to the haters.

Body Type Has Nothing To Do With It.

The stupidest part is, we are the ones that are the problem. We harbour these preconceptions based on hate and they affect how we treat other people because we judge them to be better than or less than us. Just purely based on their body type. We don't even bother to get to know the soul underneath. We just see skinny and we think Bitch or we see fat and we think Lazy. Because the media, our parents, Hollywood, society has told us that these are the preconceptions we must have. If you conform to the beauty standard and look a certain way, you will be more desirable to a mate...right?

My friend Venice says "Be kind because you have no idea what battles people are fighting underneath".

I think a way for us to honour this is to challenge our preconceptions about bodies in general. We need to stop comparing what our body looks like to how much we are valued as a person because we are so much more than just a body. Our bodies don't decide to run into burning buildings to save kittens, we do. Our bodies don't create amazing physical feats without the mind choosing too. Our bodies are tools, the patty flippers of adventure.

We aren't just a body to be judged good or bad by others because we are more than that. If we are going to be judged, let us be judged by our actions.

Do you think God thinks when they are letting people into heaven goes, "I mean they did save like 1000 people from dying on the streets but they liked the chocolate buttons a little too much so Buh Bye Y'all! Enjoy Hell ya porky wench." Our actions perceive our worth and we choose our actions and we can decide that we are worthy of love, acceptance and cake.

Saying that, our preconceptions do not come from nowhere. We see a body type, more than once, doing something we don't approve of and there we make the assumption that all people with this body type and lifestyle are the same. It is simple analytics and maths to the brain. Velma and Patrick at work.

We see jacked dudes with big biceps flexing on social media, living a happy, easy breezy life and we associate that body type with an easy breezy life. All the likes and comments of Hot Hot Hot that are in reality, really uncomfortable to receive.

Velma takes that information and Patrick applies it like a template to all future assumptions of people. But the template doesn't apply because not every jacked dude with big biceps lives in Bali, curls a tree branch and supposedly eats like The Rock but it sticks and our preconceptions build.

Like you once met an overweight person and they don't move, stay inside and are depressed. You then associate being overweight with antisocial depression and apply that template to all overweight people. And when it doesn't fit, they are the exception that proves the rule you say. Classic Jolene. She dresses revealingly, therefore she must be a harlot.

We use this information and judgements to bolster our ego or torture ourselves. "I am better than so and so because they are overweight and therefore depressed and antisocial, I am not as over weight and therefore, I am better". Or "So and So is much handsomer than I, therefore I will never have an easy breezy life and be loved".

These are the preconceptions you need to be challenging and they come from all over the place and they are bad. But don't beat yourself up for it, we all make these. We are all humans, like I have said, this isn't your fault, you are responding to the world around you.

We all have these negative preconceptions but now, I am giving you the best tool I can give you, the one that Osric gave to me.

Awareness. You Know Now.

This is all in your hands now, you have read this and you are now being faced with a choice. Face those preconceptions about what skinny means to you or what fat means to you.

Ask yourself what it means and how it actually isn't relevant to your self worth and safety. Which leads up rather politely back to other people.

Body Shaming Others

We are all part of the problem because we judge each other. It doesn't have to come out of our mouths, it can just be a thought, an intention. But allowing those thoughts to fester in your mind means you continue to think in this way that beauty is the only thing that matters and spreads negativity.

We can't control what other people do, what we can do is change ourselves. True change in the world starts within. You need to start monitoring that inner voice, the one that goes, "ugh, they look ugly today". Stop right there and take a deep breath and say internally, "we do not not do that anymore and then think of something that makes them beautiful". Then actually tell them that thing that makes them beautiful.

Involuntarily think "Oh my god that person looks ugly today" then go "Heck no, we don't do that anymore, we spread good vibes not hate" and then think "hey, their hair looks great today and oh my god they just helped that lady, how kind of them, I WILL TELL THEM HOW AMAZING THEY ARE".

This is an incredibly powerful tool, use it. What you think becomes your reality so start by stopping body shaming people and switch it to body complimenting. Don't feel ashamed by the way, we all do this. WE ALL DO THIS. But it is our choice to change, to make a difference in our life by choosing to hear that old way of thinking and changing the narrative.

Skin Tags and Blemishes

Let me tell you about Bertha.

Bertha is the large mole on my face, she grows the most majestic one hair out of it. For a really long time, this bothered me because living up to the hairless female beauty standard is a rather persnickety affair. They just pop up out of nowhere these new body issues.

I will tell a story I have never actually spoken about before.

Now, I used to live in a larger body, then one day, I lost weight and I felt like I was attractive for the first time ever (I was a young warthog back then). Do you remember feeling invincible like that? It's like being 8 years old and jumping around in the sea, true freedom. Anyway, one day, a friend of mine walked up to me and out of the blue, she told me not to worry about my "chicken wings" as she had them too.

Now, I had zero idea what she was talking about because I (and I have checked this) am not a chicken. Challenge me, I dare you. *Ghost Jade raises her fisty cuff and revs the deloren*

Turns out, chicken wings is a word for the excess skin that you have in your upper arms. Apparently (no one told me this), that we were supposed to be ashamed of this. Well, better late than never I suppose. Needless to say, seed planted, new insecurity developed that bothered me for a decade.

What has this got to do with Bertha? Well, Bertha was born the same way all of our insecurities are. We were shamed, the seed rooted and spread and the plant grew.

Your body's job isn't to conform to someone else's expectations of beauty. If someone doesn't like skin tags or moles or blemishes, that is a them problem. It is also not your body's job to look like a brand new born baby, I am sorry to tell you, it is too late for that, too much has already happened. The price we pay for living is scars, bumps, lumps and hairs poking out of moles.

If they really bother you, get them removed and be done with it. Don't waste time fretting about it, either remove it or let it go. It is easier to let it go than it is to get cosmetic surgery but it is your life. You are free to make your choices, you wonderful and majestic workhorse.

If you are a "comment out louder"

Personally, I believe in the phrase, "if you don't have anything nice to say, don't say anything at all". Especially about people's bodies because it isn't any of your business.

You don't have to comment on someone else's body just because it doesn't appeal to your standard of beauty. Life is about perspective. We all have different flavours, I get that. But remember you see the world through your perspective and your perspective, like your opinion, isn't a fact. So chill. Don't make comments. One comment can change a person's life by setting off this internal spiral so I ask you people on the internet, to just think before you speak and be kind. Even if your body shaming comes from a well meaning place, it will never come across that way. Just be supportive or don't voice your opinion, in the nicest possible way... It isn't that hard.

The "health perspective"

Oh Golly Gosh, I do hear this one a lot. "But Jade, they are unhealthy, I am encouraging them. They need to know.".

I can *guarantee* you, they already know, you pointing something out is like pointing out the obvious but with the connotation that it isn't good enough.

If you are worried about someone's weight, shaming their body won't encourage them to lose weight or get healthier, it will just make them hate themselves more and actually, you a bit.

This has been my experience in my life. Every time I have been body shamed, it has never encouraged me to lose weight or be healthy or happy or has ever made me feel like that person gave a crap about me. It just made me hate myself, reinforcing the belief that I was a failure, unworthy and disgusting. Body shaming has never led me to a good place, only to more self hate and actually, a little bit of hate for the person doing the shaming.

With body shaming, the funny thing is, it doesn't take too much to start, once a person starts the cycle, your internal brain does the rest, the relentless self hate filled rhetoric flowing around and around in your head.

And when you think you are coming from a well meaning place, it really doesn't do anything. I know you can be worried, I really do get it. But instead of criticising people, unless they are someone that it is your responsibility to take care of, it is their life, leave them to it. This can be true of wanting to protect people you love by encouraging them to lose weight because if they are pretty, handsome or attractive, then they will be safe...right? That way they don't have to suffer as you suffered. Right?

I know this can be a really hard subject to grasp because we have been raised to body shame and judge. Society holds physical appearances in such high regard that it is impossible to avoid body shaming. It isn't your fault that you are like this but it is your choice to continue this toxic pattern of behaviour. But once you start rewiring your brain to only focus on the positive, your life will become more positive. This worked for me, I don't just write this stuff down, I live it everyday. As a result of me doing this, I assume everyone else does the same and I feel really secure because I only think positive things and that energy is reflected.

Focus on love instead of hate. Instead of "I hate this about myself and other people", focus on what you love and everything else will come. The more you educate yourself the better because when you outwardly body shame, you say so much more about yourself then you do about anything else. Remember how other people insulting you is often a projection of their insecurities? Yeah, you do it too pal.

We all do. When you body shame, you announce to that person what you are insecure about and what pains you. You can learn a lot about yourself by paying attention to the words you say and speak. Once you know what you are insecure about, you can focus on healing that festering wound and finally coming to peace with the idea that your body is just a body, it is not there to impress people. If people don't like you because of your body, that is their loss.

Never forget that amazing Einstein quote:

"Insanity is doing the same thing over and over and expecting different results"

Body shaming yourself has never brought you the things you want in life, that is why you are reading this book. You can't shame yourself into a version of yourself you love. It clearly isn't working. If you want to stop hating yourself and live your best life, change tactics, choose loving yourself and your body unapologetically instead.

You are more than just a body. You are funny, interesting, passionate, wild, square, dorky, sexy and chaotic and we love it. *Ghost Jade does a little dance*

Activity: Complimenting Tornado

Go out and compliment someone's body each day and your own. And when a compliment comes back, accept it gracefully (or as gracefully as you can, not so graceful in my case) but either way. Smile and say thank you.

If you are feeling up to it, up it to several people a day. It is called the complimenting tornado because eventually you just endlessly compliment and it is amazing.

Speaking of complimenting tornados, I haven't told you today that you look fantastic and you have a wonderful face. You are whimsical and radiant and I love your vibe. Whatever you are up to today, I hope you have an exceptional day, you beautiful soul.

STANDARDS OF BEAUTY

I want to talk about where all these toxic thoughts about your body come from because and I quote this a lot:

"If you know the enemy and know yourself, you need not fear the result of a hundred battles. If you know yourself but not the enemy, for every victory gained you will also suffer a defeat. If you know neither the enemy nor yourself, you will succumb in every battle."

– Sun Tzu, The Art of War

Know thy enemy. Beauty standards are the enemy so let's dive into it shall we.

The idea of beauty is a social construct and a malleable one at that. It means we decide what is beautiful. Our idea of beauty is defined by external factors, by our environment, we are told what is beautiful and it changes with every passing decade. Do you know the saying "Men always marry their mothers", it is because they experience what love is and they think that is beautiful.

Every passing year (now thanks to social media), the idea of what we see as beautiful is designed and orchestrated by businesses who want to sell you things. They decide, create products to sell to you and then they promote the coconuts out of it.

This is very important, very loud and proud. I want to say this.

Other people's opinion of your body is none of your business.

If someone doesn't like your body, that is their opinion. Most of the time it is rooted in:

1. Societal ideals of beauty and they are just parroting the same crap they always see.

2. They have suffered too. They are reflecting their own self hate onto you. When someone says a comment about how your body isn't good enough, It Is Not About You. They are projecting their pain and trauma onto you.

If someone doesn't like your body, that is their issue. Your body is still beautiful, wonderful and amazing. If someone repeatedly tells you that your body isn't good enough. Ask them to stop, bro down style and be like, "those comments aren't helpful to my mental health, please stop".

If they persist, cut them from your life. You don't need that negativity in your life. Sometimes it's a partner, sometimes it's your mother. It may be a shit friend or a co-worker (throw back to toxic relationships). If you ask them to stop making comments and they continue, that is bullying. Don't be afraid to stand up for yourself. Well be afraid cause we are all but do it anyway.

The more we stand up for ourselves and defend our bodies, the more people will be inspired. By standing up and being brave, another person will feel empowered to do the same and together, we can create a movement and create massive social change so that this won't even be a problem in the future. Be the change you want to see in the world.

Now back to the main event. Society's beauty standards.

Society, my old nemesis. The thing about society is... It is a liar. Until about 80 years ago, for woman it was sexual and fashionable to be curvy, skinny women were prescribed fat pills to bulk them up because it was shameful to be skinny. Then they realised that actually, the ratio was around 10:90 for naturally skinny people to curvier people and some fancy man in a top hat went.

"Wait a minute. We're only cashing in 10%. If we just made skinny attractive and shamed curves.. Think Of The Profits." *insert dollar bill signs in his eyes*

So they did.

Magazines started with weight loss tactics, skinny models and newspapers reported new creams and pills to help them look a certain way because of course, it is a womens job to be beautiful and please her husband. *Ghost Jade rolls her eyes*

This was a lucrative business so they went on and thought, "okay, how can we profit on this more? I know. More problems that we can fix. Cellulite? That naturally occurring thing? Get rid of it with this product."

For men, it has been even stranger. In all the old movies, it was always an older gentleman who was just snappily dressed. Then we had Marlon Brando and Elvis and it spiralled from there until we have the beauty standard that is forced on you today.

You see, society's standard of beauty doesn't care about you or your mental health, it is a profitable machine fuelled by magazines, celebrities and movie stars all with the same body type that sucks on your self hate and turns it into DOLLA BILLS Y'ALL. How many times have you seen the article of a Marvel actor who bulked up for a role and is now winning awards for looking attractive? How much was Thor fat shamed in Avengers End Game?

This ridiculous body standard of square jaws, 6 packs, beards or you look like a Timothée Chalamet with perfect genitalia size because apparently that has to be standardised as well. (It's how you use it, I am just saying). Women may get a lot of the heat but men are struggling just as much as women. All bodies struggle if I haven't highlighted that enough yet. Just because small white bodies are represented in the media doesn't mean you guys aren't subjected to the brutal beauty standard because no matter what body you are in, it isn't good enough for society. Because if it was, then they couldn't profit off you and as we have established, dolla billz y'all.

The beauty standard is relentless. You have to be tall but not too tall, skinny but not too skinny, hench but not too hench, 10 abs with no ass but also a big ass, big lips but not too big, you don't want to be too pretty, that's gay. Nice eyes but not like that, look young but not too young, but not plastic, it has to look natural. 6 packs and square jaws, no body hair, bleach everything but also be tanned in all the right places. But do it classily, don't look too trashy or people won't think you are worth anything.

It is a brutal standard and they use fear to enforce it. Using racist and homophobic comments and toxic masculinity, they isolate you so you think it is only you who is struggling and then they overwhelm you with content so it becomes harder to fight back.

No one meets up to this standard and if they do, they were photoshopped to look that way. It is also just one image. Just a snap. It's not a reflection of someone's actual body. Then it is shoved in your face 24/7 through the media which is more and more accessible so at every given moment that you aren't living in a cave, you are subjected to the beauty standard. It is physically impossible to meet this beauty standard.

It is time to let go of this, time to let go of the idea that you will be beautiful in the eyes of society. Let it go. Breathe. You are still handsome even if you don't look like the dudes on the magazine covers. Doesn't mean you can't be handsome, accomplished and successful. Since beauty is a social construct created by our environment, it means you can choose what you think is beautiful.

There isn't just one flavour of ice cream. Don't get me wrong, vanilla is an amazing flavour, but so is strawberry, cookies and cream, vegan mint choc chip and mango sorbet (I am a mango sorbet myself). Just because the world we live in promotes that only vanilla ice cream is the only delicious flavour, doesn't mean that it is the flavour for everyone. Even if it is available in every fast food restaurant ever, just go to nicer ice cream parlours.

The media uses the unrealistic beauty standards to keep the business of beauty alive but that business only thrives if we let it.

We give power to what we give attention too. If we pay attention to it. If we read their body shaming articles and buy their products.

Here is a fun fact (not too fun if you aren't a nerd like me but here we are). Did you know that when Julius Caesar was murdered, in his will be left 75 drachmas to every citizen of Rome? You may think "that was nice of him to leave every man some money" and it was. But it was also tactical because he was buying the loyalty of every citizen of Rome for his successor, Octavian. Because Caesar knew the fundamental truth, he who controls the mass, controls the world. Whoever has the army and the people on their side, will control the country.

We need to pick our leaders wisely and I am not talking politically here, I am talking about the content you consume, the people you pay attention to.

Have you noticed that when you have those hate spewing celebrities that everyone hates but they are always on the front page, vomiting up racist and sexist controversies and you just think "Oh God I have to hear what they have to say again".

Here is my theory and it totally works by the way, if you ignore them, they go away. The media makes money through attention, the more attention you give it, the more money they make. If you take your attention and spend it elsewhere, the media will have to adapt. If enough people start ignoring the hate spewers and focus on the positive role models, the world will change. Another fun fact, a long time ago, I researched how to help people experiencing a verbally racist attack on a bus, the suggestion was to go and sit with the victim and talk to them and pointedly ignore the racist.

They can't tell us we aren't good enough if we don't listen to what they have to say.

Photoshop 101

We touched upon it a little so now it is time to talk about it a lot. Photoshop. The tool that has been helping Velma and Patrick reinforce toxic beliefs about what your body should look like since 1987.

Bodies represented in the media are almost always photoshopped or edited to be more "aesthetically pleasing". I am not going to lie to you or to anyone, the enhancements they make, look better. Of course they do. But do we think that because of how we believe beauty should be and what they look like?

I don't mean to start an existential crisis for you and question what even is reality as we know it, I just want you to understand and question the reality of your world a bit. What you see on social media isn't real. Even if it's your friend posting an unfiltered photograph of themselves. That is a snapshot of their life, it is a moment, positioned and posed. It isn't real. You cannot compare yourself to posed snapshots you see online.

As we have discussed several times, it isn't your fault. Your brain is much faster than you can comprehend. Velma and Patrick work in tandem, they work when you aren't even paying attention and Velma, they are smart, they can think tiny thoughts for Patrick to file away so the belief sneaks up on you.

You can feel really good about yourself and then scroll on social media for 5 minutes and suddenly start thinking really down on yourself. Because Velma and Patrick have been watering the plant of self hatred and where did they get the watering can from? Yep, you guessed it, photoshopped images on social media.

That is why it is so important to make sure your feed is filled with things that bring you joy but eventually you are going to have photoshopped images of people. You might even see me on social media and those thoughts may start popping, if they are, refer back to chapter 1. We don't compare anymore. We are a team. We are both beautiful, we are both worthy and we are both awesome.

To avoid the world of photoshop skewering your idea of what bodies should look like, we are going to talk about body envy in detail.

Envy

We are processing some ugly emotions during healing which brings me to something that when I first talked about it, I got a lot of shit for. Personally, I think I am just ahead of my time because people love to sit and pretend we are all so evolved and perfect but the reality is, we have to deal with things like body envy, we can't have the body we have always wanted, it can be hard to see people who have so let's talk about what we can damn well do about it. I won't leave you hanging.

Since we are human and as the movie Inside Out demonstrated, we have the ability to experience envy. Body envy is something that no matter how body positive you are, no matter how much you love yourself, it is something you are going to experience. Because you are a human. *Ghost Jade envies Brooke Ence*

Let's begin with why.

Body envy is a form of comparison specifically, downward comparison.

"Research suggests that we're more likely to make downward comparisons when our self-esteem is threatened—for example, if we've just received negative feedback—because these comparisons give us a boost, enhance our own perceived standing, and reassure us that things could be worse".

Who are we comparing ourselves to? Who is the benchmark?

To everyone it is a little bit personal but it looks something like the Chad I keep alluding to.

Meet Chad. Chad is 6 foot, 0% body fat but with a cracking chest, curvy butt, 6 pack but not too muscular, just a bit of definition. So much hair on the head but zero on the body. Tanned to perfection. Not a wrinkle, scar or an imperfection in sight. Think of the most beautiful person you have ever met and then photoshop them. It is normally something like this, something that your peers go "Oh My Gosh, they are so hot/beautiful/righteous and make all the people gush". Body envy is for all genders.

This is mostly thanks to our age old "friend", the Media. They pick what is beautiful, photoshop it and then shove it in our faces and then invent products to make us "look like that". The media created hate for our bodies and then profited on it. Then they say things like "Oh people must know this isn't real" and I am like. No. I didn't know they were photoshopping images in the 80s. I thought that was only invented a few years ago (dunce moment) but the point still stands. Young people do not know that what they are looking at isn't real or attainable.

But I digress, back to you because then it goes something like this:

You are doing you, just living your life. Being chill, being wholesome and handsome. Maybe you are eating nutritionally and doing your best and you are feeling pretty good.

Then you flick on social media and there it is a beautiful person. Maybe they are eating something delicious, high in calories, abs for days and looking amazing. Maybe they are just living their hashtag best life, doing amazing things like living in Bali making millions on Instagram. Maybe they are successful in other ways, have a successful career, 3 kids and still models for Vogue on the side and make their own perfect wedding invitation.

There are many of them in many versions and they are all personal to you. It could be the house dad, with his #1 best selling book, works full time and still runs the house, cooks healthy and makes all the time for his kids. It could be the CEO, 10 abs, perfectly tanned and jacked makes millions a year. Or it could be Hugh Hefner, you do you. It could be your friend who has everything you want. It might be Chris Pratt. Whatever your comparison triggers, I am sure they are beautiful and unattainable (maybe because hey ho, you aren't actually Chris Pratt).

And your brain goes, "fruitcakes, I am not good enough. It's because they are beautiful in the eyes of society. I don't look like that, therefore, I am garbage". And then Envy sets in.

Envy doesn't make you a bad person, in fact, as established at the start, it is human. Now my natural reaction is to be like "shame your body Jade, look at you, you flabby sack of snacks". Then shame in another way and be like "No Jade. Be better than this." I want to break down the process for you because there are a lot of things to consider.

Process for dealing with body envy, I will do my best not to repeat myself too much but a lot of the fundamentals are the same.

Remind yourself that you are good enough
Let's deal with the fact that this image or person made you feel not good enough. They have what you want and now you feel like what

you haven't isn't enough and that simply isn't true. Just because someone else has a different life and prioritises, doesn't mean you have no value. You are a wonderful, beautiful and vibrant person and your body doesn't reflect that. Your body is just a tool for adventure, bring it back to gratitude and reground yourself in the reality that you are good enough.

It isn't real
You see a photo it may not be photoshopped but it is perfect lighting, perfect pose. I know because (as a size 14 girl), I managed to position myself so it looked like I had a flat stomach and a cracking rack. No one posts their scruffy photos and let's be honest, even when they post their authentic pictures, they are still the best of a bad bunch with a filter. My sister is a smart lass, she taught me positions and poses to look good in images and it is fine, great even to post your best pics that make you feel like a queen on the gram. But know that it was one good picture that was carefully crafted out of potentially hundreds of images. What you are looking at is a nice picture, but it shouldn't affect your worth in any way.

Set your own standard of beauty and have it nothing to do with body type
As we have discussed, beauty is subjective. You can decide that beauty is found in action and kindness and not in a body type. You can also decide that curves are beautiful or you are one of my beautiful slim friends, you can decide that your slim body is beautiful. You can decide that you are beautiful no matter what society says because society doesn't control you, you do.

Remind yourself that all bodies are different and your body is beautiful and amazing just as it is.
You can appreciate a lovely body without devaluing your own. If you resent or hate someone or body shame someone, that only spreads negativity. Look at them with love and say, nice body, mine is great too. We may look different and we may live as if divided but we are

all the same, a human who is just looking for happiness. All bodies are beautiful, no matter what.

Deal with your feelings about food. Don't restrict yourself.
When I see fitness models eating like kings and eating shitty food it makes me feel like my body type is garbage. Restricting foods you love only leads to bad juju and when you do so, it only leads to food envy or Food FOMO. Nothing bummed me out more than seeing a fitness model eating food I wouldn't allow myself (normally sugary treats) because I don't want to "Get Fat". But I am an old goose now and I allow myself anything I want and as a result, I get less food envy because I could have it. Also, let us also remember that these are snapshots of someone's life, literally photographs or moments. They may not even be eating the food they posted on social media. Don't compare yourself to someone else's food. It's a waste of time.

Control
You can't control if someone likes you, you can't control if someone doesn't like your body. That's not your business. You can only control yourself, your choices and how you behave. If someone doesn't find your body attractive, that is their business. The only business you have is making sure you like your body and focus on all that you have and not all that you are not. You are not perfect and in that imperfection, you are perfect. Because you are alive.

Focus on what you can control, not trying to win over other people's admiration and approval, but focus on yourself and your life. Focus on treating your body with respect and being body positive. Reassuring yourself that you are worthy of love and respect. Because you are. If I haven't made that abundantly clear then I am not doing my job right and yes, I am happy to repeat this again and again because it is key.

Gratitude for your body
Have gratitude for your own body. I say this so much it is my catch

phrase, your body is a tool for adventure, it is not an object to be adorned. You don't have a body to impress other people with its ability to conform to social norms. Your body is built for you to breathe, run, dance, work, create new life. Your body is built for you to reach for cookies on high shelves and build nano technology that can build a better world. It gives you the dexterity to pick things up with your toes and squirt milk outta your nose. Your body isn't a precious painting, it's the paintbrush and life is your canvas. Treat it with the love and kindness it deserves.

Tell your body you love it.
You have no idea how much it needed to hear it. I always say treat your body as if it were your child, do that. Self care, express love to your body. Honestly, when I first did this organically, I cried because it was so impactful.

Focus on you
Don't focus on what they are doing and what they look like. Bring your attention back to you, your life, your goals. What do you want to do? What do you value? What do you want to do with your life? Let go of what they are doing and bring your attention back into your lane. Make sure the Velma is focused on all the great things you are doing.

We all sail in boats
Understand that even your friends that trigger your body envy, have issues of their own. Everyone has body image issues, no matter how beautiful you perceive a person. We are all struggling with it so don't blame or throw shade on other people for having what feel your self worth is threatened by. Be kind always. We are all in our own boats travelling the river of life. End Body Shaming. Appreciate a body and appreciate your own. We are all beautiful in our bodies.

Comparison Mindset

We briefly chatted about this but it's time to come full circle. Let's talk about the metaphorical knife you keep stabbing yourself with and talk about comparison. It is ruining your life.

Comparison is the killer of joy and most importantly, the killer of good body image. When you compare yourself to someone negatively, you focus on the idea that you are not enough just as you are.

You are enough just as you are.

You may not be for some people but that is their problem. If they don't appreciate you for who you are, that is their loss. You are a unique, beautiful, amazing and vibrant spirit. I have always been comparing myself to others who were popular and accepted and finding all the ways I was weird and different because I never seemed to conform to society's ideas of normal. But the thing is, we are unique. All of us. Society created this one role, the role of the damsel in distress and if we didn't fit into that role, we weren't good enough.

You aren't comparable. It's just a fact. You haven't walked in anyone else's shoes but your own so the only shoes you should be focusing on are your own.

I have a theory. At the gym, I used to compete with people and I used to cut down my workouts or reps so I would finish sooner than everyone so I wouldn't feel like an idiot that's fat, slow and crap. Until one day, I did just that. I completed a workout at heavier weights than everyone and yes, I finished 20 minutes later than anyone else and it felt amazing because I didn't compare or compete, I focused on myself, my journey and my growth. I died and was reborn from fire. I smashed that workout.

To avoid a long story about fitness, don't compare or compete with anyone because the only person you should compare yourself with is who you were because that is where the satisfaction is.

Don't be thrown off by other people's success, use it as inspiration to keep going because one day, someone will turn around to you and say, "holy crap, I wish I were you". If I believe in anything, it is that we should stop comparing and beating each other down for an ego boost and start lifting each other up.

There is a super cute post floating around on social media that says "Queens don't hate, Queens adjust each other's crowns".

That is the whole premise of this book, this book is to help you lift your crown back onto your head so you can reign supreme in your life like the King you are.

Don't compare crowns, be inspired, support and rule with an iron fist. One day, many people are going to turn around to you and be amazed by how "instant" your results are and they won't see your journey. By the way, there is nothing more annoying than people assuming all your hard work learning to accept your body, grow confidence and love is down to luck and not down to your hard work.

But you get to shine your way through and help them lift their crowns and it will be glorious.

Ageing

Bodies change and bodies age. We can't fight it, it's natural. Your body ageing is the price you pay for living.

From the get go, we are afraid to age. We can't wait to get to 18 or 21 so we can totally be adults and do whatever we want. Then we hit those ages then it's terrifying, like we are taking one step closer to the grave every year. Every passing year mocks us as we become less interesting, less handsome, less worthy, less everything.

We have been taught that being young is beautiful. How many times have you heard the term "don't waste your youth" or "live while you are young"? We obsess, buy products and surgeries to make sure we stay looking young. Because if we look young, we are attractive, we have value. Even though at the time, we didn't feel like that at all.

Because the beauty standard is unattainable.

I can't stop you ageing and you know what, I don't want to. It's happening whether you like it or not but you can choose to see it differently. You can focus on all the ways you are ageing and changing and think "Oh Lord I am disgusting, I will never look young again, no one will ever love me again".

Or

You can choose to see yourself for what you are and say "I am ageing and it is beautiful, I am older and wiser and attractive because getting older doesn't mean I am not sexy and awesome and worth loving. It just means I have been lucky enough to live this long."

It isn't your fault, have you noticed that most villains in movies are either fat, old or of colour?

We are all ageing and in this world where businesses are desperately and relentlessly trying to convince us that we are supposed to look young forever.

"Look at Paul Rudd, he is redefining what you should look like at 50".

That is a genuine headline I read once and I thought to myself. "No, that is just how he looks, that is not how every 50 year old is supposed to look. A person is supposed to look like what they look like". Can you imagine if you went to the local shop and everyone looked like Paul Rudd? That would be really weird and extremely boring after a while (no offence to the wonder that is Mr Rudd but we are all cherries on a cake).

You forget, most celebrities have access to the fanciest and most expensive plastic surgery to keep the natural process of being alive at bay. *Ghost Jade pays no attention to celebrities and trashy magazines so she doesn't know if Paul Rudd has surgery or not. All we know is that he is beautiful and so are we*.

Did you know by the way, that in France, it is considered attractive for a woman to get older? In America and Hollywood, it is attractive for men to get older but in France, it is women. Isn't that interesting? Reinforcing the reality that your ideals of beauty are created by the society you live in and not what you actually think. Beauty is fluid.

This is a really long way home way of saying, you are going to get older. It is a luxury not afforded to everyone, don't hate it. Love it. Love how beautiful your parents look, admire how amazing your wrinkles, your speckles and your human toe beans look. (I'll let you work out what human toe beans are).

You have a beautiful body. It is powerful, wonderful, amazing and incredible. There are plenty of people in the world who are going to say bad shit about your body but you should never say it about yourself. Because let's be honest, how many people to your face or even online have directly told you that your body is horrible? I know that people have but not in a very long time. But and this is where we get to diverge and specialise just for you guys because men love to Banter. I love a bit of banter, don't get me wrong but I want to dive really deep into another particular issue and how to deal with it.

Height

Death to the height stigma.

This really chaps my ass this one because whenever I say anything, I get my height thrown back in my face. I mean it is no secret, I am snack sized. Reaching for the cookie jar requires a level one in climbing.

But height insecurity is just another body issue. You are worried that your height affects how you are perceived. This is why books like this have to be general because not everyone will have this insecurity. Personally, I don't because I look fantastic in a pair of Dr Martens (and so do you!) but a lot of men struggle with this beauty standard that you have to be 6 foot tall to be attractive.

If this is you, use the tool from this book. What are you afraid of? What are you ashamed of? What would you want if you could change your height? What is the real goal here? Can you get this without changing your height?

Unless your life goal is to be able to reach cookie jars on high shelves, your height doesn't often impede on your life. And if your life goal is tall enough to reach a cookie jar, just get lower shelves, achieve it and then find another life goal.

Your height doesn't affect how attractive you are, how worthy you are or how beautiful you are. Sure, you will get some potato who judges you based on height. I mean.. Tinder is a minefield of humans who are forcing the beauty standard onto you.

Here is my advice from someone who loves all heights of men.

You can't change your height, so accept it and find someone who finds it attractive too. Don't try and date people who are never going to be happy with your height.

Don't just date people who are shorter than you for the ego boost. You are missing out on some awesome tall people you could be dating, if you let go of the height insecurity and realise that all heights of men are awesome. You are epic, hot, awesome, smart, cool, fancy and wondrous regardless of your height.

Hair

Let's talk about a real issue that affects most men, a vast amount of men. Balding. Because of the toxic beauty standard (You know I feel really bad for anyone called Chad, this is why Karens get upset about their stereotype), the Chad look, they always have a full and majestic set of hair. In male banterous culture, you mock each other for a lot of things because it's how you show love, I get that but also, sometimes those banterous things turn from funny to hurtful.

There is a strange deconstruction here I want to do.

What are you afraid of if you lost your hair? Or have you lost your hair?
What are you afraid of?
Not being attractive? Not being accepted?

Fear is a sneaky snake. When someone mocks you for something you start to wonder "Oh, is this something that could actually happen? Should I be more worried?". Fear sets in, you could lose what you have, you might never get what you want, you might never be cool.

It always comes back to what do you want from your physical presentation.
What are you afraid of happening if anything affects that?

168

And how can you bring it back to a feeling of safety.

Because people will still love you, romantically, sexually, friendshippily and familially. Your worth isn't held by the amount of hair you have on your general head. The beauty standard has set that you have to have a full set of hair and be able to have a full and majestic beard, just in case you need it. If you have that, you will be attractive, you will be beautiful, you will be successful.

But (and hear me out) how many successful, happy, rich, cool, awesome, smart people don't have hair?

Your happiness isn't dependent on your hair. Your happiness is dependent on your attitude towards your hair and hair loss in general.

Changing this all starts with why are you afraid.

If you dig deep down, it is the raw fundamentals of change. I am afraid this change is negative and I will lose something. If I lose my hair, my partner won't find me attractive anymore. I am afraid people won't take me seriously if I don't have hair. I am worried I will get mocked and I am getting old.

Firstly, you are getting older, we have another chapter for that. We are only going one direction no matter how much the beauty standard, pharmaceutical companies and the media are trying to convince you otherwise.

But I can help you let go of the fear.

You are an ever changing person, blooming and growing. Letting go on old ideals and growing in your next phase of life. Last season was all about cars and parties and maybe this season is about travelling and one on one experiences with someone special. Maybe next season is discovering you are allergic to pomegranates. One is not less valuable than the others, we are all part of this amazing cycle of our lives and just because it is perceived as cooler to be in a previous season, doesn't mean it is. Your identities come and go as your seasons change.

You need to embrace the season you are in now, season 7: the body acceptance and buying the right size jeans for once. It isn't the snazziest title but hey, season 7 is always a top season. You are heavily invested in the characters and they have levelled up the antagonist so much that everything just becomes comically absurd.

Which brings us to fear because the big bad guy in your story is the expectation you put on yourself to conform to the unrealistic masculinity standard. The Chad Energy (again, so sorry to all Chads).

The pressure to be a Chad is what is causing the main issues with your hair right now. We have hair, sure. It is nice when it's all poofy but it isn't where your worth starts and ends.

Why are you afraid of losing it? You are still you without it. Having nice hair is an identity that you can let go of.

You will be okay with it.

Let Chad energy go and understand that, no matter what. You are loved. You are cool. Coolness is not found in what you look like, it is found in who you are and what you do.

Case and point, what is cooler?

A guy dressed in fancy clothes, standing by a concord, looking candid, drinking a beer in the sun.

Cool right?

Or

A guy snowboarding down a mountain to escape an avalanche because he was filming content for national geographic.

That is dope.

I am just saying, if they cast Harrison Ford as bald for Indiana Jones, we would still love Indiana jones. We don't love him for his hair, we love him because he's so cool.

Worrying about something you can't control is only leading you to misery. Don't spend time worrying people don't like you, don't waste time worrying how you would be perceived poorly. Compensate, be Indiana Jones. Be awesome by your actions, not by your looks.

You will pick up way more dates as well, you are welcome.

From a Ghost Jade point of view, I once went on two dates (spooky dates) in quick succession. One guy was like princess perfect hair and all. The other guy had no hair, bald with a dope hat.

From an insecurity point of view, I logically should have dated dude number 1 right for a second date? Because having hair means you instantly score with the ladies... right?

Or.....

I dated the guy who was funny, charming, brilliant and fun. Amazing how his hair had nothing to do with that.

Plastic Surgery

You might think because I think you are gorgeous and you should accept your body as it is, that Ghost Jade is against plastic surgery. I am not, you do you. It is your life, your choice, your world.

If you want to change something because there is no way you can accept it. For example, you were bullied about your nose growing up and you just can't let it go. No matter how hard you try and the trauma is just too embedded. Why not? If you can afford it, do it.

I believe you don't have to change your body to find whatever it is you are looking for because what you are looking for probably doesn't require an aesthetically pleasing nose. But I do believe if it is hindering your happiness and it is something you want to do. Heck, you do you.

Don't be ashamed of your life or your choices. Save the shame for when you do something really stupid and you need to apologize.

You are wonderful, beautiful, cool, awesome and spectacular.

Friendship 101

Okay, it is easy to let go of the fear but how to stop taking it to heart when you get mocked for it. Because everytime your friends mock you for hair loss, they are saying (to your subconscious), you aren't good enough, you are a loser, you suck.

They don't mean that, they love you. If they didn't love you, they wouldn't say it. One thing I learnt in Australia, if someone calls you a friend and is nice to you, they ain't your friend, they hate you. If they call you a word that sounds like buntcake, you are their BFF.

You don't have to change the way you communicate with your friends to stop your feelings getting hurt. You just need to take the fire power out of their guns so instead of hitting you with bullets, they are hitting you with blanks and then eventually, they just have water pistols. A gun fight is not a good time, blanks are still painful and fatal but everyone loves a water pistol fight.

How are we going to do that?

Understand that unless your friend is a malicious butthole, they don't mean to hurt your feelings. Most of the time, your friends are projecting their insecurities and fears onto you via insulting banter. When they say something (this applies to most body issues by the way), they are often saying "I too am concerned about this issue and I wish to feel safe".

People are really simple when you break down the fundamentals of how we communicate. We are just animals experiencing our life in different ways.

If your friend is a malicious butthole, please refer back to Toxic Relationships.

It is important to note that your friend isn't responsible for how you feel. If you aren't communicating that it upsets you and ask for it not to be mentioned while you process and let go of the idea that you have to be a certain way to get what you want in life, how are they supposed to know?

If someone banters, you feel insecure about it, just breathe. They don't mean it the way you are taking it (if they do, let them go). Take a moment to remind yourself that you are more than your appearance and they are just projecting their trauma onto you. You are still cool, awesome, brilliant, smart, outstanding, beautiful and kind. Just laugh it off and remember that no matter what anyone thinks about you or your body, it is a tool for adventure. Not a tool to impress your doofus friends, they are gonna like you for your personality, not your looks.

Which brings us in a round-about way to the final aspect of letting go of body image issues, grief.

Grief

Heck yeah we are going to talk about grief. We have talked about many topics by now but we haven't talked about a realisation that you may never look the way you have always envisioned, obsessed over and dieted towards. You've been obsessing over looking a certain way for so long, coming to terms with the fact that you are actually, fine as you are and you don't have to look like that to get the things you want in life. That can be a loss. You can grieve. First thing I learnt at funerals is everyone grieves differently which means, you need to take a moment to let go and grieve.

Let's talk a little about the grieving process because I always find that helps me when I have experienced a loss.

The basic 5 stages of grieving are:
- denial
- anger
- bargaining
- depression
- acceptance

You might be at any stage and you will keep going through them. Have you noticed when you experienced a loss like a break up or a death where you feel like you are getting past it and you are moving forward and then something else pops up and you feel like you are back to square one. When you lose something, it is often multifaceted.

For example, you don't just lose a romantic partner, you lose a friend, someone to do certain activities with like pebble collecting and you may process losing the romantic element but then you have to process the next loss in another area of your life and you restart the whole process over again.

You feel how you feel. The worst thing you can do is tell yourself how you should be. There is no should be, there is only what is. Even if you are someone who doesn't enjoy expressing your feelings, taking time to process them is important.

What really helped me was realising that I am the size I am supposed to be and there was nothing wrong with that. I am what my body wants me to be and just because that isn't skinny, doesn't mean it is wrong. It took me a really long time to grieve the loss of the idea of who I should be but then I realised that I can be exactly who I have always wanted to be in the body I have now. In any body because who I am is not my body.

You can do anything you want to do in your life. You are an outstanding human being. You are funny, kind, brave and wild even if you don't feel it. You are so much more than you think you are. You are capable of anything and I believe in you. 100%.

Activity: Judgement Day

I do this every now and then. Go to your local store and just look at the magazines. See past all the marketing and see it for what it is. Advertisements to sell you products. Little booklets to tell you how you aren't good enough. Pity them and instead tell yourself that you don't fall for their pretty little lies anymore. Inoculate yourself against their toxic messaging. Practice makes perfect.

This was a long topic but it could be a book on its own but the key and most important thing to take away from this chapter is that beauty standards are subjective. They are created by businesses and promoted by the media to sell you products. Your ideal of beauty can change when you decide that actually, all bodies are beautiful.

No matter what size, shape, age, ethnicity, color, sexual orientation or ability.

You get to choose that and when you decide to love your body and let go of reading toxic articles that body shame celebrities or diet tips. When you decide to stop paying attention to idiots and instead of fueling the fire, just be thinking "oh lord how embarrassing". You get to choose that the beauty standard is what it is, a giant sales technique for a product you don't need. Because you are beautiful regardless of what your body looks like and not everyone will see it but that's okay. It isn't your job to prove your beauty to other people, your job is to love yourself.

You are attractive by the way. You have a beautiful body, it is amazing, sexy and dope. You are praiseworthy and definitely worthy of being adored and worshipped as a God.

THE COMMUNITY

Let's talk about the body positive community because this is a very female heavy community. It may be scary and feel like as a man, you aren't really welcome there. But, I intend to change your mind on that with my classic candour. On your adventure through the theme park, there are diverse types of rides and hot dog stands, one are solo kart rides and some require a group of you to walk through a haunted house. Welcome to the BP Ride. It's wild and it is time to find you people.

This is a community of people who want to celebrate all body shapes, from color, to queer to size, all bodies are too be celebrated.

They want to encourage all people to love their bodies no matter what shape, age colour, ethnicity, sexual orientation, gender or size. I find that amazing and I love this community.

It's not just for plus size or fat people (words recently reclaimed by the community), it's for everyone. Here is a little bit of background for you.

"The fat acceptance movement was pioneered in the 1960s by black and queer women to fight discrimination in public spaces. The workplace and doctor's offices. Fat positivity, which is more of a reaction to fat shaming and body positivity, which is more of a commercial self-esteem movement came later.

The body positive was first created in 1996 by Connie Sobczack and Elizabeth Scott and trademarked by Debora Burgard in 1997. From there, a beautiful movement and community flourished. Since then, we have had loads of body positive activists, models, artists all pop up and encourage and influence people to love their bodies."

This is where it gets complicated because the body positive community can be very passionate and I never felt that I, in my small white body, never really belonged as I am in love with fitness and eating natural and a supporter of athletes, models and people wanting to change their bodies, it is your body you know? Do what you like. A lot of activists and models feel like they are betraying the body positive community by wanting to lose weight.

The BP community gets a lot of shit because like most things, there are a faction of people who take it too far. I know for me, I hate drama and I don't like shaming any type of person unless they are an asshole but I get it. If you have a space where your body type is finally being represented and it's being taken over by bodies that look exactly like unrealistic beauty standard bodies. More Thin White Bodies, you'd be pissed too.

But that being said. Body Positivity is what you choose it to be, it's about what we have talked about, loving yourself, your body, not judging people and embracing your beautiful body as it is, no changes needed. The community is there if you want it. It is a huge and thriving community and they are an endless source of inspiration. I couldn't be prouder of everything they have accomplished because I wouldn't be writing this book without them.

Let's quickly go over some key words for you that I found helpful when I first ventured into the fold.

Body Positivity: Body positivity refers to the assertion that all people deserve to have a positive body image, regardless of how society and popular culture view ideal shape, size, and appearance.

Body Acceptance: Body acceptance is defined as accepting one's body regardless of not being completely satisfied with all aspects of it.

Fat Acceptance Movement: The fat acceptance movement is a social movement seeking to change anti-fat bias in social attitudes by raising awareness among the general public about the obstacles faced by fat people.

There are so many subsections of this community to explore. As you may have noticed, this book is called Body Acceptance not Body Positivity because I am an antisocial old goat who would live in a cave if it had access to wifi and a bed and a kettle. I drink a lot of tea. The point being, this book is about accepting your beautiful body to be what it is, a tool for adventure. It isn't about other people, it is about you. Control what you can control.

Activity: The BP Community

So really for an activity, the plan really is to just go out and find them. FIND YOUR PEOPLE. Follow channels and activists on social media, find local groups. Find people who love to talk about it and share their wisdom and communicate. They are out there, you are not alone in this fight. Go be inspired as I was.

The BP community is amazing and so are you. You are epic, beautiful, awesome, smart, funny and accepted. You are welcome and there are people out there (like me), who are so excited to welcome you and tell you how amazing you are.

Because you deserve it.

SEX AND BODIES

This may make you uncomfortable because full disclosure, it would have made me uncomfortable but this whole book is supposed to make you feel uncomfortable so get used to it. It might not be relevant to you by the way, if you are asexual, still a youth or you just aren't that keen, feel free to skip!

This is actually a hilarious chapter to write because when I wrote it originally, it was a lot more targetted at letting go of your shame and enjoying sex. I didn't even think to cover the male perspective where you are forced into being hyper sexual as part of culture. So instead of focusing heavily on embracing your sexual nature and not being ashamed of it, we are also going to talk about letting go of these performative needs which means, we have to talk about porn. Sorry. This will get uncomfortable for you.

Once again however, we have to get some basics out of the way.

I have to call this out right away, I would love to advise better but I am actually demisexual (which means I don't experience sexual attraction to people unless there is a deep emotional bond).

Seriously. Which means talking about sexual attraction is difficult because I like people for who they are, not what they look like. To make this easier. If we are in a bar and you look at an attractive person and go "Oh my god, they are attractive, I would love to have The Sex with them", I will nod and wingwoman (of course, I am an excellent wing woman) but I cannot comprehend doing it myself because they look like a grey andrygonous blob. Everyone is a grey andrygonous blob to me. Which means everyone is beautiful to me, unless you are an asshole. My perceptions of beauty are built on who you are, not what you look like.

As a result, body attraction isn't something I can comprehend which is why I don't feel best informed on this topic. Which means, you may have to venture out into the unknown. However, as we are loving of all sexualities, this means it is open to all the genders and sexualities. Normally, my sexual orientation wouldn't matter much, like my particular feelings around croissants but if I was writing a blog post on the best croissant place in Paris, it would probably come up that I hate crossiants.

Anyway, grab a croissant and let's dive into something I learned back in 2014.

"Unattractive people hook up with attractive people all the time."

This baffled me as I am sure it will baffle you. You always think to be successful sexually, you have to look and perform a certain way. A way I am sure you don't feel you can ever be like. Don't get me wrong, if you are confident in this area, treat your partners with respect, be safe, make sure you both consent properly, move on to the next chapter.

But for the rest of us, the point is that we have this idea that if you look like the beauty standard, then sex, confidence and happiness will come easily to you. Because you are "deserving" of it. No one ever told me that I was allowed to be considered beautiful, attractive or sexy. No one ever bothered to mention to me that just because I didn't look like a supermodel, that didn't mean that people didn't find me attractive.

Mind blown so I thought I would share this little nugget of knowledge with you.

You are sexy. You are hot. You are allowed to feel those ways. People DO find you attractive.

We value so much on other people proving this fact to us. For example, we don't get hit on in bars, therefore, we must be unattractive (we talked about this with our belief systems, our brains find proof to support the belief that we are unattractive). Or we have been rejected one too many times and it must be our bodies fault, if we just looked better, people would be more receptive to our pheromones.

Yes, I will continually try to make you laugh through this adorkable chapter.

Other people shouldn't have to prove that you are attractive, you already are. No proof required.

Which brings us all the way back around to permission. I give you permission to be sexy in the body you have. I give you permission to enjoy pleasure and sex and whatever you fancy. I give you permission to love your body or even just accept it. Now if you could give it to yourself, that would be amazing!

And another sneaky secret? Confidence is sexy. The more confident you are, the more you will get attention.

Permission done, you are attractive and you don't need other people to validate that. It can be frustrating when you want to date someone but they don't like you for sure, I like to believe it is because they weren't meant for you. The right person will get you. Anyway, let's talk about body image and how porn has messed with your head.

Body Image and Sex

I'm going to say it. Pornography has skewed our perceptions of sex. It was bad enough they were shaming us in the streets but they are shaming us in the sheets?! Is there no part of our lives that are free from the relentless and brutal standards and expectations for us to conform to. Even if you don't watch it, it is hard not to be affected by the "should" of how you should look and what you should do with sex.

I will say it, there is no one way to do anything, especially sex. Sex shouldn't be about performing to look aesthetic, it should be a messy, raw explosion of feelings and pleasure.

Guys, for you it is much worse. Women get porn but you are subjected to porn from a very young age and you are conditioned to act and perform like porn stars. You are pressured to do things, be hyper sexual all the time, be aggressive about it and take what you want. From my experience, that hasn't been true with most men. Most men just want to connect with their partners in a more intimate way. But the hang ups created by the porn industry stops them from letting go and enjoying themselves fully.

But (and bare with me), it's like comparing yourself to a movie character. Not an actor and a body but like a movie character. It is like comparing yourself to Luke Skywalker. You want to be like him, do the things he does but at the end of the day, you don't have a millennium falcon and you don't live in space. Because it's a movie character, that isn't real life. He also makes out with his sister which is just a bit weird if you ask me.

Activity: Stimulation

Next time you find yourself in bed (alone or with someone) and you are feeling frisky, take some time to discover pleasure without shame. No holding back. Unless you are breaking the law or someone else's consent, focus on how you feel. Let go of the performative nature and just follow what feels good.

I am going to say this because I hear this A LOT from the people I help. People are inherently selfish. Focus on pleasing your partner, educate yourself on their body, what works for them. Study them.

Make them want to get down on one knee and want to only worship your body forever. Part of that is working out what works for you, so make sure you do that activity.

This must be the only homework you have ever had where someone has gone, grab your dick and lets go but hey, the world is an amazing place.

Performance issue and penis size

Oh yeah, we are talking about the Chad Penis size issue. Lucky for you, you are reading this and you don't have to sit in public and squirm while a woman explains to you the very simple and basic logic of "It is how you use it that matters". Because it is, it ain't that complicated.

Now my wonderful men, you are all wonderful and different sizes. You come in all ways around the rainbow and we love you for that. You might be hetrosexual so you might not understand the appeal but I want to explain this from a woman's perspective. I mean lets be honest, apart from urinating, no one sees your BFF unless things are getting a little spicy in the sheets. Intimacy is where it matters and size does not apply to this.

Ghost Jade "I can't believe I am giving a lecture of sex, what has my life become"

If you want a rewarding sex life where your partner isn't dissapointed, it isn't about the raw materials you have to work with. It is all about how you treat your partner, how you communicate, finding what they like, how they work, what their kinks are.

To put it bluntly, you can have a micro penis and still give someone the best night of their life. Sex isn't like it is in porn, where you just jam it in their and a person does some moaning and bam, orgasm city. Those are movies. If I was to raise my arm and fire a particle beam out of my mechanised gauntlet, nothing would happen because I am not actually living in a Marvel movie.

If I was, I would rock the superhero vibe. *Ghost Jade wears a spandex pair of pants and a mask, staring majestically into the middle distance*

If you are insecure about your penis size it is because you are worried about being judged. For not being good in bed, not being able to perform, not being able to satisfy, not being as good as previous partners.

Want to fix that? Educate yourself on how to give your partner pleasure. Find out what you like, experiment. Try new things and let go of the performative nature of sex. You don't have to go through steps and make certain noises and say certain things like you are acting out a script. Your life isn't a movie, it isn't porn. No matter how cool Iron Man looks staring down Thanos, if that was us, we would crap our pants and run. It is just a fact!

Your raw materials are just that, raw materials. Sex is a huge topic and lets be honest, if you are struggling with porn addiciton, performance issues or other more serious body/ penis related issues, there are professionals you can go too. Ones who know a lot more than me about how to help you through a deep issue. All I am saying is to let go of the fear of failure and fail your way to success. Learn how to create pleasure and practice, fail, laugh when it gets awkward and try again.

Sex shouldn't be a perfectly orchastrated affair where you are getting from point A to B. It should be taking the long way home because your first date is going so well and you just aren't ready to stop chatting to each other yet. It should be unexpected, unplanned, raw, authentic, messy, sweaty, smelly and full of failure in the best way.

Don't blame what you got, work with what you have. The more you practice, the more confident you will be.

That is my homework for you, go do some research and have sex with a nice consenting partner.

Ghost Jade shouts to your retreating back "DON'T FORGET TO COMMUNICATE AND PRACTICE SAFE SEX"

Activity: Letting go of Shame

I have an activity for you, grab a notebook *Ghost Jade throws a notebook at you*

If you are struggling with feelings of shame about enjoying sex or not wanting to have sex as much as society thinks you should, how your body looks, performative insecuties, whatever shame is holding you back from a thriving sex life. Here is an activity I wrote to help you let go of those feelings.

We are going to let go of the feelings of shame we have. We all feel ashamed about stuff, I mentioned our secret shameful guilty pleasures but shame can go much deeper than that. What are your biggest disappointments in yourself? What Are You Ashamed of? Body image and sexually speaking but please use this for any other ways you feel shame.

Grab the notepad *Ghost Jade tosses a pen at your head*

Write down all the things you are ashamed of cause we are about to cross them off the list.

1. Accept that these things you are ashamed of are a part of your life. They are who you are and you like them and there is nothing wrong with that, maybe some people won't accept them but if it brings you pleasure, it brings You Pleasure. Your pleasure is more important than their approval.

2. Your past transgression that you are ashamed of, they are in the past. This can totally be awkward encounters and those memories that make you cringe. Forgive yourself for your past and move forward. Your mistakes have helped make you Who You Are. You had to fail in order to learn. Your mistakes that you are ashamed of are a part of you. They kept creating you, moving you and building you into the person you are because you learned from them. You aren't perfect, let it go.

3. Own it. Just own it. Your flavours, your desires, your interests. Don't be ashamed of who you are, take responsibility for what you enjoy and what rocks your socks.

Let it go, empower yourself. You are supposed to be you. You are supposed to love the things you love. Enjoy them. No shame.

Communication

If you feel insecure about your body it can make any kind of sexual activity really uncomfortable and I don't have to explain this to you, you may know. You have to communicate with your partner. Lack of communication is the cause for most of life's woes. You have to be upfront about what you like, what you want, what you expect and what makes you comfortable.

Also, reassurance goes a long way. There is nothing worse than being intimate with someone who doesn't assure you that they are enjoying themselves and find you desirable. Make sure that you are communicating to your partner and they are communicating to you, that you are having a mutually enjoyable experience.

You deserve a rewarding and thriving sex life but because it is such a taboo subject, it can be really hard to not only talk about but learn about. The more you know about your body and what you like, the happier you will be.

Love Languages

Since we are talking about communication, you should know that people communicate in different ways to express love.

The 5 are: words of affirmation, acts of service, receiving gifts, quality time, and physical touch.

Every man I have ever told this too and snorted in my face derisively, then done it, realised how they and their partner communicate differently, then adapted and their life became amazing. Communication is important in every relationship you have, including non romantic/sexual ones. Knowing how you communicate and how your partner communicates means you can enhance the experience 10 fold. If your partner prefers words of affirmation (aka compliments) and you prefer quality time (aka snuggles), working together, you can both have an amazing time. So before you snort in my face, do it, change your life and then never thank me for it, just do it.

You can do a quiz to find out which one you are and it will help you. If you are with a partner who expresses themselves via gifts, it can be frustrating if you value quality time instead and it can lead to misunderstandings and miscommunication. Learn what your style is and what your partner is so that when it comes to expressing love with your body. You know what works for you and what works for them. This is another form of refining your communication skills, you may have a partner who shows love through gifts and buys you toys and outfits for you but you express love through quality time so you may prefer just a long foreplay and a cuddle after.

It is time we take the shame out of sex. It isn't something to be ashamed of and everybody that wants it, deserves it. Make sure you do that previously noted activity every now and then. You will be amazed what pops up.

Dating

I didn't want to include this section to be honest because what can I say really? You are going to date, people suck and dissapoint. You are going to be rejected based on what you look like. Thanks to the tinder era, there is even more pressure to be Hollywood Perfect. Aka Chad. It sucks but the good news is, most people are suffering together.

But then you find someone who really works for you and it is amazing so here is what you need to consider when dating in the world when you accept your body for how it is.

I am going to tell you what I tell everyone because these are gender free rules for life. Do not tolerate disrespect. Seriously. I mean it. I know your low self esteem means you let people walk all over you or you keep going back to toxic people for a little bit of a boost. You cannot tolerate disrespect. (Remember, disrespect and constructive feedback are different, you might be being a dick, you aren't perfect and that is okay). You deserve to be with someone who values you, you make you feel great about yourself. You are not a feral raccoon, don't go eat out the trash cans. You are a well groomed, well raised raccoon who eats birthday cake at home and loves berries.

We talk a lot about domestic abuse in the world today but it goes both ways.

If someone doesn't respect you or your body, then leave. There are plenty of other people who will see your value and worth. This journey towards self acceptance, it is a wild roller coaster ride (remember, you are at a theme park), this is just another one of the rides. Don't get on the roller coaster with someone who is going to throw up on you and blame you for it. Go find a partner who totally vibes with you.

The most common thing I get from people who find me and need my help is people who need to leave relationships where they aren't valued. Romantic, friendships, work wise, no matter what, they find me. The one thing I always tell them is that they are beautiful and they deserve better. Dump their ass, go on holiday and be free.

Because you deserve to be appreciated, loved and made to feel sexy. No Matter What Your Body Looks Like.

This was relationship heavy, remember, we don't judge, we love a promiscuous human. You do you! We don't shame and we are sex positive here. Just make sure you are being respected and appreciated and if not, ditch them, find someone worth your time.

Flavours

I have always said I have no flavour, I like people of all bodies, it is what is inside that counts. I live by that, I date around the spectrum but I do know, I have a specific taste for a certain flavour of a person that my personality finds attractive. Lord knows I love a spicy woman. There is nothing wrong with being attracted to certain body types, that's just how flavours go. You can like your men shredded and your ladies curvy. But you don't fall in love with someone because they are hot. You date them for that and you fall in love with them for who they are, their flaws and perks.

Don't be ashamed of having a certain flavour of person. But do know that people are more than they appear, don't disregard someone because they don't appeal to your idea of beauty. Don't be put down if someone doesn't see your beauty because it doesn't appeal to them. Just move on, they aren't meant for you and have some faith that the person who is meant for you is out there. Or 2, or 3, there are 7 billion people. Plenty of choices.

This is the most untalked about topic in body positivity and body acceptance but it isn't something to be ashamed of. Remember, we aren't ashamed of who we are. We are awesome. If this is something you are really struggling with, there are so many resources out there for you if you know where to look. Sex therapists exist for a reason.

Now this isn't my area of expertise as mentioned because of my sexual orientation being on the asexual spectrum but I was struggling with poor body image, intimacy and feeling the need to be performative rather than an active participant. This really helped me and If I could summarise it for you into one sentence it would be:

Communicate, neither you or your partner fake orgasms and for Lucifer's beard, know your worth. You are gorgeous and sexy goddammit. If someone treats you like you aren't good enough, dump their ass.

You are unapologetically hot, sexy and awesome.

You are attractive. Sexually if you are into it. You are beautiful and pretty and handsome and attractive. You are mesmerising and anyone would be more than lucky to have you. You are the most amazing person and I hope you know that.

Because I believe it with every ounce of my soul.

Part Four:

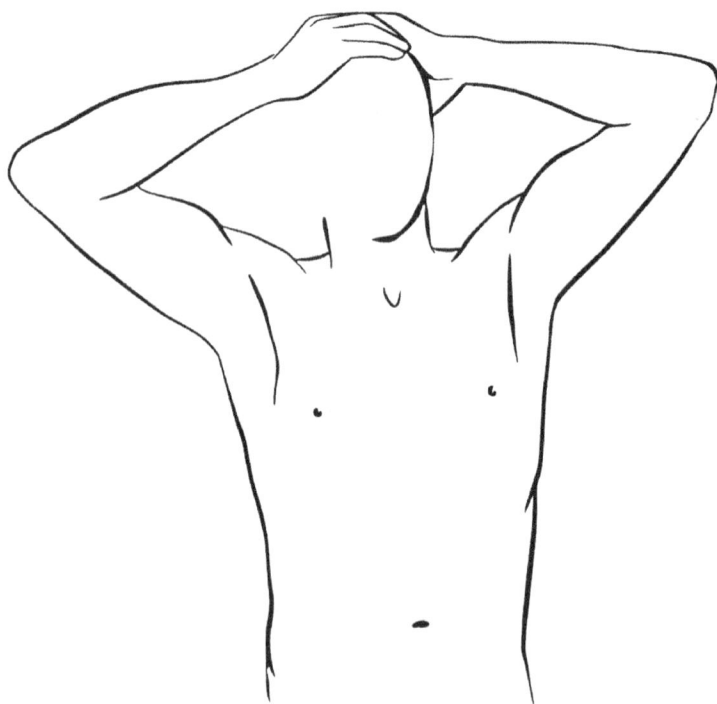

Changing Your Actual Life

CHANGING YOUR ACTUAL LIFE

If you have made it here! THANK YOU! I am honestly so happy you have kept reading through my book. This final section is all about a recap because I have done a huge information dump on you and now I want to clarify the action plan.

Because you can read about something all the livelong day, but ideas don't make change, actions do. Now you have done the reading part, maybe tried some of the activities (I know I wouldn't, that is why we have this bit), we can start on the Action.

You have one shot in this life, how do you want to spend it? Regretting? Dieting? Hating yourself? Apologising for who you are? Not doing things you love? Chasing approval from people who can't see your value?

Or do you want to believe in yourself? Take risks. Be brave. Do what feels awesome.

If you want to change and accept your body, I mean really accept it. You have to get off your butt and commit. Choose to change.

You have one shot in this life, make yourself proud.

PERSONAL
RESPONSIBILITY

Entering Savage Territory, I warn you now. You know now. You *know* that your body is a tool for adventure. You **know** that your body's job isn't to conform to unrealistic beauty standards. You *know* that is a tool to experience life with.

We have to talk about Personal Responsibility.

When you blame someone else for your problems and insecurities, you place control of your life into the hands of someone incompetant. We do it so freely, we put our bodies, our self worth and our body confidence into the hands of others.

By saying, it was their fault. You say "this bad thing happened but it's not my fault because I don't want to feel unsafe. I also don't want to take responsibility for this incase it comes down badly on me." But it is time.

TO TAKE RESPONSIBILITY FOR YOUR LIFE!

FOR HOW YOU FEEL

WHAT YOU SAY

WHAT YOU DO

Stop thinking someone owes you anything. Not your parents, not someone you've brought a lot for. Nobody.

Stop relying on someone else to make you happy, only YOU can make you happy, other people are there to make you happier, not happy.

Never forget, the person who broke you can never be the person who fixes you. You have to fix yourself.

Be afraid because you are afraid and do it anyway. That thing you are most scared of that you're avoiding facing because you are afraid of rejection or pain. Do it. Face it.

When you mess up, apologise and say "OH MY BAD GUYS SORRY" and forgive yourself because I already have forgiven you. We all mess up. It doesn't feel like people will forgive us because we are pushed to be perfect but hey, guess what? We ain't.

Take responsibility for your life, your mistakes, your choices, your trauma, your bad habits. It is not your parents fault you hate your body, it is not your other parents fault you hate your nose. Sure it may be the cause and that was rude of them by the way but the continued habitat you maintain for it to fester in, is on you. You keep telling Patrick to water the plant. People aren't perfect, they are flawed and they say things without thinking and have no idea of the torment you are putting yourself through day in and day out. But you can choose to change.

Own your life. Be brave. Baby steps, when you think thoughts like it's her fault I feel like this. Correct yourself. No, this is on me. What can I do to change this pattern of behaviour and thinking? How can I take back control?

Take a deep breath and forgive yourself for making that mistake and move on.

Own it, let it go. Be afraid, do it anyway.

It is **that** simple.

"Okay Jade, JEEZ, Relax. How do you do it? Because that is totally not something I am used to doing and I am afraid for so many reasons". Great question my friend.

When blaming other people is easy and no one wants a failure to come down on their head, making people think we aren't good enough, competent or skilled. This is a leadership thing, you have to have that mindset of lead by example.

Personal responsibility means when something goes wrong, I don't blame anyone, I take responsibility for my part in it. No hate, no shame, just saying, this was on me, sorry. The more you can take responsibility for your actions, the more control you have. You don't put control of your life into the hands of others, which is what you do when you blame someone for something.

1. Take responsibility for your thoughts, feelings, words and actions.

These are on you, no more saying, "Oh I was just drunk" as an excuse to be an asshole to people. No more, "I said it while I was angry but I didn't mean it", you meant it. If you don't want to deal with the consequences, maybe just don't say it outloud. Be kind and keep your opinions about others in your safe brain zone. Think whatever you want, but you have no right to ruin someone else's day with your opinions.

2. Stop blaming and Stop complaining.
You can bitch and moan for 5 minutes, then you gotta get back and change the narrative in your head.

3. Refuse to take anything personally

Stop assuming that everything is about you and taking any disagreement as a personal attack. *Ghost Jade holds a sign saying "When you Assume you make an Ass of U and Me*
Remember, you don't have control over how other people respond, you only have control over how you respond.

Most of the time, it's probably not about you, but about the issue at hand. Instead of making assumptions, ask the question, is this even about me? If it is great, how can you take responsibility and grow? If not, don't take it personally. Remember, it's not about you.

4. Make yourself happy
Self care people. You have to make yourself happy, that is your personal responsibility. It is a lot easier to love and accept your body when you are living your best and happiest life. That starts with doing shit that makes you happy. Even if that doesn't conform to the expectations set by society.

5. Live in the present moment and live intentionally
We talked about this, let go of the past, forgive it, focus on what you are grateful for right now.

6. Practice Confidence
Confidence is a practised skill and by practising taking responsibility for things, you will feel more confident in it. Which means, when the big things hit, you can ask, how can I be responsible for this, how can i adapt or improve to change so this doesn't happen again in the future.

You are smart, we know that. You are exceptional. We know that. We know that you are beautiful, kind, generous, spicy, passionate and adventurous. We know that you are you and who you are is amazing.

So I will leave you with this thought. You rock and you are cool and I dig your vibe. You are smart, zesty and valued.

HOW TO LOVE

YOUR BODY

Welcome to the effective recap of this book. Firstly, if you made it here, holy macaroni, congratulations! You put up with all that crazy talk, bless your soul for being so kind to yourself that you were willing to read this book to attempt to help yourself grow, change and be happy. Now that is out of the way, let's go.

To love your body is to experience freedom. Freedom from doubt, self hate and oppression created by you.

To love your body is to no longer hold yourself back from what you deserve.

To love your body is to grow and enjoy your life.

Self love is a necessity if you want to live a truly happy life. Self love is a choice, a commitment to yourself that you are going to love yourself, despite all the social and biological obstacles in your path. It is not found in a place, person or item.

What Do You Need To Do To Love Your Body?

1. Choose it

Self love is a choice, it isn't handed to you. It is not found in someone else or in an object, you achieve self love by deciding that you want it. After a lifetime of hating yourself and your body for not being enough, you have to choose to let go of this toxic mindset. Choose to say no to all the internal self hate and choose to tell yourself the truth, that you are not perfect and that is okay.

You have to choose to love yourself. You have to choose to love your body. You have to give yourself permission to love yourself and love your body.

You have to decide to choose love because no one is going to do that for you. No one can do it for you, no one can walk this journey that you're about to walk on. You're about to go on an abundant hike into this wonderful world of self-love and acceptance.

No one can carry you through it.

You're the one that has to put in the work.

You're the one that has to walk down the road.

You're the one that has to take the steps and you have to choose and you have to keep choosing it every day.

When someone makes a comment, you have to choose to love yourself.

You have to choose to put in the work and you have to choose to reach and head towards that place of complete acceptance and love.

Even when you get there, it's so easy for someone to just go, nope or for you to just go and relapse back into your own negative ways.

You have to fight and you always have to keep choosing it.

Choose to love yourself and your body and your life because you deserve it. You deserve that peace.

Give yourself permission to love yourself and your body. You are worthy of being loved, even if you tell yourself you're not. Take a moment to tell yourself this and give yourself permission to love yourself and your body, this is the first step in accepting that you can love yourself and that you are choosing it.

2. Achieve self acceptance

You are who you are and there is nothing wrong with that. You don't have to be something else to have worth or to be good enough. Who you are right now, is enough.

People may not like you and that is okay because the point of self acceptance is that it doesn't matter what other people think of you, it only matters what you think of yourself and your body. That starts with accepting that you are who you are and having faith that there is nothing wrong with that.

I've got a big imagination (as you may have noticed with the bats in the belfry) and this was what I was thinking about the other day.

When I was younger, I always wished I could just switch bodies into someone else's body entirely. I would rather have lived in a thinner, smaller, white, perfect body with big boobs than live in my own body.

I thought about it and wondered what if that came true?

What if I then switched bodies with another person? Their mind went into my body and we would be switched.

But what if it was across different realities and we couldn't switch back. I had everything I wanted right? Everything I ever dreamed of that I would trade anything for. But I could never go back to my body or my life (this is what I think about in the middle of the day on a random Tuesday).

Then I mused, what would I miss? What would be the things I would struggle with the most?

Because I would have this perfect body that I've always wanted. Would I be happy when I have everything in life I wanted and what would I miss the most?

The thing I thought of was that I would miss looking in the mirror and seeing my own face. Not because I had any love for my face but because when I look at my face, I can see my sister's nose and my mother's eyebrows and my father's hair.

I see my brothers and my sisters and my family and I see my life etched into skin. I see myself and my life and I would find it so difficult to live in another body and not be able to see my family in my own face.

And as time went on, I would forget what they looked like because, you know, my memory's not great. I thought that's the saddest possible thing.

We spent so much of our lives wishing we were in different bodies but imagine if the cost was that great.

I thought I would share that because we always dreamed that we could be in different bodies and we never appreciate things that we have right now.

We have beautiful, amazing functional bodies.
We have amazing people in our lives that love us.

And they all go and so unappreciated because we would rather have this perfect body. I just think be grateful for what you have in your life, in your body and sure, it doesn't conform to society's expectation of beauty.

But you know what?

You've got so much good in your life that is going unappreciated.

3. Know that self love is an endless journey

As we go through life, we grow, change, learn and become entirely new different people. We are all different people to who we were 10 years ago which means self love isn't just learning to love yourself once.

It is about falling and being in love with yourself and your body as you change and grow. You don't achieve self love, you travel with it as you discover who you are.

I'm going to shoehorn in something here that I don't have to but I'm going to anyway and that is your limitless ability to express love.

People often think that the love that they have is limited and that is because they give out love so frequently and so easily that they often feel emotionally drained, overwhelmed and exhausted.

Making them feel like they have no more love to give.

I want you to think of your love like the water that comes out of your taps, like it's limitless. You can literally fill up a hole like a swimming pool with it.

Although the well is limitless, you can't carry the tap around with you so we fill up little watering cans of love with us in our hearts.
We are happily pouring our watering can love into everyone else's pot plants to make sure that they're growing and thriving.

Then it's empty and you're like, "oh, no, there's no love left for me, it is okay, I was unworthy of it anyway. If anyone cared, they would have watered my plant". Exhaustion creeps in and you feel unloved and worthless. You give too much away my love before you go and refill your watercan. And you can refill it at any time, just take it to the tap and fill it back up.

Take a break and refill it.

Sometimes that can be through socialising or it can be through going into the forest and not talking to someone for two weeks.
However you recharge and re-energize that is refilling your watercan of love.

You have to remember to water your plant to make sure that when you are off in the world being an amazing person, make sure you water your own plant. Water your own plant first. They say put on your own life vest first before assisting others for a reason. Water your own damn plant because you can, you should and you have to.

4. Let go of the idea of perfection

You are never going to be perfect, no human is. Don't let that stop you from loving yourself and your body, it is easy to hate yourself and your body for not being perfect or enough. But this only creates self hate because instead of focusing on all that you have, you are focused on all that you are not.

Self love blooms in a mindset of abundance, which means you have to see all that you have and feel gratitude for it. Self love struggles, wilts and dies in a mindset that is rooted in perfection aka never good enough.

5. Identify the difference between Truth and Opinion

Self acceptance starts by changing the way you think and see yourself, this all starts in our internal talk and the stories we tell ourselves.

An example of our stories would be:
"I can't do this because I am too..." Something like thin, fat, short, ugly.

These stories come in many forms, such as:
"I cannot have this in my life because..", "I am not good enough, this is not meant for me. If I looked like this, I could get what I want. I would deserve it then."

"I am..." Insert negative adjective.

Taking a good hard look at your internal rhetoric can be really revealing as to why you have struggled to love your body.

When you are down on yourself, if it is because at some point in time, someone or something made you feel not good enough. It could have been a comment from a family member, a judgemental magazine article or a random video you watched. It made you question your worth and you took this knowledge and used it to hate yourself.

What I want you to do is realise that most of these thoughts aren't facts, they are our opinions of ourselves but we treat these opinions as facts. Irrefutable facts. When we tell ourselves we can't do something, we won't, it is a self fulfilling prophecy. Which confirms in our brains that our opinions are facts.

When you say I cannot or I can't or this isn't meant for me, you kill 2 things.

1. Hope, you decided you cannot so there is no reason to try.

2. Growth, you cut off the opportunity to try, fail and grow.

You become stuck in a fixed mindset with no choice but to succomber to your fate as a self imposed loser. If you want to love yourself, this needs to stop because these aren't facts. Let's break this down to the basics.

A fact is a thing that is known or proved to be true.

An opinion is a view or judgement formed about something, not necessarily based on fact or knowledge.

For example:
It is a fact that an orange has a peel.
It is an opinion that the orange is round and therefore unattractive.

Let me translate.
It is a fact that you have fat on your body.
It is an opinion that having that fat makes you an unworthy person.

It is a fact that you are skinny.
It is an opinion that having that body shape makes you unattractive.

We give power to facts and we can decide if it's positive or negative, self destructive or empowering. It is time to let go of these opinions and change them. Instead of "I cannot apply for this job, I am not qualified". Make it "I can apply for this job, although I am not qualified for it, I can always try! I will always learn something and that is always fun".

6. Learn that failure is your friend

When we fail, we use that as an excuse to hate ourselves for not being good enough but you have it all wrong.

Failure is growth, instead of focusing on how we aren't good enough, focus on what you learnt. How did you grow? How can you apply this knowledge in the future? The faster you fail, the faster you grow!

Don't let failure be the reason you hate yourself, choose to love it and laugh at yourself when you fail. Laugh, get back up, think about how you can grow from this and move forward. You are going to fail a lot in your life, you might as well have it on your side and when you do, it will grow and foster self love.

We live in this weird world where we have a lot of overnight successes and a lot of successes are constantly thrown in our faces.

Like weight loss is a great example of this but business is also a fantastic example of this.

They'll be like "this overnight business started".
I would be like "that's so successful, it's because, you know, they're lucky or they're skilled or they're magic. That can happen for them because they're special and different, but it can't happen for me".

But what you seem to forget is that that overnight business was actually ten years of hard work and dedication and failure.
Every successful person will tell you it is failing your way to success.

You have to fall flat on your face and get back up.

That is what success is.

You have to understand that failure is your friend. You have to fail in order to experience growth and happiness. Happiness comes hand in hand with falling on your face.

You know what?

Here with my best and stupidest example for this Burpees.
(A burpee is a squat into a press up and they do a press up and then you come back up into a jump). It is a horrible, exhausting movement and everyone hates it.

Everyone also hates failure and I always attribute the two because if you do burpees they become so much easier, I would say almost enjoyable. Failing works the same way.

You get fitter and you become more successful. You have to understand that failure is essential to success and happiness.

Every time you get knocked down, pushed over or someone makes a rude comment or you just get back up, if you find yourself going down a negative spiral, understand that you fail, that's fine.

Get back on the horse.

You have to learn to get back up to rebound and be like "oh, I failed. Great. What did I learn? let's go!".

Having this failure is my friend's mindset that can change your life because instead of looking back and thinking "oh, look at all the times I failed. You'll be like, actually, look at all the times I grew. Look at all the things I've learned in my life so I can get here so that I can go here and I can achieve everything I wanted to achieve".

And I no longer have to worry about the shape of my body in order to do that, because it's good enough and worthy enough just as it is.

This is actually something you can practise, pick something and go and attempt it and fail. Try again and again. It doesn't have to be giant and scary, it can be something as simple as making a sandwich. Practising everyday to get closer to prove to yourself that you failed once but persistence is key.

And I no longer have to worry about the shape of my body in order to do that, because it's good enough and worthy enough just as it is.

7. Learn how to not take things personally

The thing about life is, it isn't all about you. We are bombarded with negativity and most of it, directed at us, we find ways to be offended as well, not consciously but we do. This is biology at work but now it's time to let go of this defence mechanism.

How do not take things too personally

1. Know that the comment that has just hurt you, isn't about you at all. See it from the other person's perspective, 50% of the time, it isn't even about it. It can be redirected aggression or maybe, you were just there.

2. It is about you and you need to show yourself some empathy, be vulnerable and kind to yourself and talk in a non blaming and judgemental way to the person that has offended you.

By not taking things personally, you stop find new and wonderful ways to not torture yourself and therefore, love yourself because not every negative thing that happens isn't about you. The world is bigger than just you.

Let's discuss when someone makes a negative comment about your body.

It is not about you or your body. It is them displaying their toxic view of bodies At you. It's not about you, you are just, unfortunately, in the way.

I love this because it kind of clicked so naturally in my head, like all of these terrible bad things have happened to me.

I would always blame myself and my body because I take responsibility for stuff. I would blame myself and take fault for things not working out or causing their bad behaviour even when it was so out of the blue.

And I realised it's not about me.

If some people just don't like you, it's not about you, it's about their insecurities and their toxic beliefs and they take it out with you because sometimes you're just what they want to be and they can't understand it.

Love is the perfect example for this.

I love my body. It's nice. It's a good body. It does great things. It dances. It has been found that hairy legs are kind of hilarious but a lot of people hate that I love my body.

I lost quite a lot of friends I had in my life because I love my body. People don't know how to deal with this because of envy, insecurity or confusion. Powerplay comes into it, people who use you as an ego boost by asserting that they are better than you over you. When the truth is outed that that isn't the case and actually, you are amazing but not better than anyone, they lash out. They take out their aggression and their opinions on you. It's frustrating and it's upsetting but you have to understand that it's not about you.

It never has been about you. It's about their stories and it is about you.

If they're making a genuine critique, you just go "thank you for your feedback. I have learned and I will apply this in future"and see if it's actually relevant to you, if it can actually help you grow. If it can, wonderful. If someone is just being asshat, you could just ignore it and move on with your day.

It is important to understand that 100 percent of negative comments about your body have nothing to do with you.

If some bozo has walked up and said "you know, it's unhealthy to live with that body, you know" and you are like "oh, yes because you care SO much about my health, a random person I've never met".

8. Start the discussion of body issues with other dudes

We have to move forward with this. You have to start talking to each other about your body issues. I realise toxic masculinity means that you can't express vulnerability at all, meaning expressing you are struggling with something opens you up to attack.

I know, it is scary and painful. But I don't mean just starting with talking to random people about your issues, I mean start talking to your friends about what you are dealing with, see what they are dealing with and share solutions. I think that is why women get problems solved pretty quickly, because we discuss our issues, listen to others suggested solutions and apply them if necessary.

Did you know that humans developed social skills, so much so that we were able to win over neanderthals because of our ability to gossip? To communicate.

Our ability to communicate is our greatest asset. Use it. Talk to your friends, your male friends about what is going on, how you feel. If they don't take it seriously, that is fine. Just find someone on your eave length, someone else in Chapter 7 who is looking to grow and change. It is a fascinating subject and it is an ever constant journey to listen to people's thoughts and insights on the subject.

You are the most exceptional person in your life. You aren't just another person. You aren't nobody. You are one in a billion, billion (yeah I said it). You are amazing in infinite ways, you can literally do anything you want to do in your life and I will cheer you all the way. You are without a doubt The Shit as the kids say these days.

PUTTING ALL THIS INTO PRACTICE

Let's talk about activities and moving forward. You have read this book! Thank you again! I appreciate it! You are amazing!

Recap time! We are going to go over all the major activities I want you to do and what you can do moving forward on your adventure into body acceptance.

List of activities

Activity: Name 3 things about your body that you are grateful for.

This is simple and straightforward, you don't have to say it outloud, just think of 3 things right now. Thank your body for keeping you alive. You are reading this because eyeballs are amazing.

Activity: What If?

What is it that you will achieve if you finally hit that "Body Goal"? Now write out how you can give that to yourself.

Activity: Pick The Word

Pick a word, an adjective about how I intend to approach the week. It can be Brave, Productive or Kind, Rest, Chill Out. Pick a word that represents how you want to face the world today.

Activity: Permission

Give yourself permission to love your body

Sit down and make a conscious effort and do whatever you need to do.

If you want to write it down, declare it on social media, do a spell, buy yourself a new pair of I give myself permission pants. Whatever comes naturally to you. Do it. Give yourself permission to accept your body as it is.

Activity: Myths and Legends

I want you to write down myths that you have about your body and then you basically dispel them.

Activity: Pick The Word

I love this activity, I do it weekly. I pick a word, an adjective about how I intend to approach the week. It can be Brave, Productive or Kind, Rest, Chill Out. Pick a word that represents how you want to face the world today.

Activity: Man-ual Maintenance plan

Yes, I did name it that for that one pun. Write a list of all the things that make you feel great about you, things that are important to your self care and print it out. Make it easily accessible so that you can easily reference it for the days that you are paralytically stuck in your own head.

Make it pretty, easy to read and then make a weekly and daily routine that works for you and do it

Activity: Go as you mean to go on.

Clear up your life. Your environment, your social media, your inbox, your friends, your life. Go as you mean to go on.

Write down who you want to be, what you want to do and what kind of people you want in your life and start to make those changes. If you don't know where to start, clean one room and buy a pot plant. Feel the reward and then repeat, clean up and replace it with something that provides nothing but love.

Activity: Gratitude Daily

Everyday, I want you to think of something you are grateful for about your body.

Write it down, say it outloud, say it to someone, post it on social media. Whatever your process is, thank you body for its service.

Activity: Get Out Into Nature

Once a day, spend 5 minutes a day outside in nature. No screens just you and the trees or sea or wind.

Activity: Complimenting Tornado

Go out and compliment someone's body each day and your own. And when a compliment comes back, accept it gracefully but either way. Smile and say thank you.

Activity: Judgement Day

I do this every now and then. Go to your local store and just look at the magazines. See past all the marketing and see it for what it is. Advertisements to sell you products. Little booklets to tell you how you aren't good enough. Pity them and instead tell yourself that you don't fall for their pretty little lies anymore. Inoculate yourself against their toxic messaging. Practice makes perfect.

Activity: The BP Community

Go out and find them. FIND YOUR PEOPLE. Follow channels and activists on social media, find local groups. Find people who love to talk about it and share their wisdom and communicate. They are out there, you are not alone in this fight. Go be inspired as I was.

Activity: Stimulation

When you find yourself in bed (alone or with someone) and you are feeling frisky, take some time to discover pleasure without shame. No holding back. Unless you are breaking the law or someone else's consent, focus on how you feel.

Activity: Failure

Pick something and go and attempt it and fail. And try again and again. It doesn't have to be giant and scary, it can be something as simple as a yoga pose. Practising everyday to get closer to prove to yourself that you failed once, but persistence is key.

Resources moving forward to start with:

Social Media Influencers
@bopo.boy
@drjoshuawolrich
@gentlemenscurb
@stilashlee
@kelvindavis
@mattchuupicchu
@Zachmiko
@extra_inches_plussizeblog
 @realryansheldon
@kennyethanjones
@guyoverboard

Books
Body Positive Power: How to Stop Dieting, Make Peace with Your Body and Live by Megan Jayne Crabbe

Happy Fat: Taking Up Space in a World That Wants to Shrink You by Sofie Hagen

Things No One Will Tell Fat Girls: A Handbook for Unapologetic Living by Jes Baker

Food Rules: An Eater's Manual by Michael Pollan

Health at Every Size: The Surprising Truth about Your Weight by Linda Bacon

Landwhale: On Turning Insults Into Nicknames, Why Body Image Is Hard, and How Diets Can Kiss My Ass by Jes Baker

Body Kindness: Transform Your Health from the Inside Out--And Never Say Diet Again by Rebecca Scritchfield

Podcasts
Unshaming
The Silent Battle: Men, Body Image, and Mental Health
Affirmation Pod
Living in this Queer Body
She's All Fat: A Fat Positive Podcast
Break the Diet Cycle
Fat Girls Club
Bad Fat Broads
Food Heaven Podcast
The Recovery Warrior Podcast
Body Kindness
Nutrition Matters

You are awesome and you rock! Go and continue being wild!

CIAO BELLA

WELCOME TO THE BEGINNING OF YOUR LIFE!

With every new end, a new door opens and you can begin your life anew. With the end of this book, I hope you open the next door to the next phase of your life. The phase of self love, body acceptance and so much more.

The journey will be arduous but it will be gosh darn it worth it. This book is meant to be a stepping stone on your adventure into the unknown, I said at the start, body acceptance is like visiting a theme park, this is just the park map, it is time for you to get on the rides and try them out, see what works for you.

Thank you so much for making it all the way through and for being here. I am so grateful that you've made it this far and I'm so grateful that you've started your journey to accept your body because your body is beautiful, amazing, wonderful, awesome, cool, fun and sexy. No matter what, no matter what size, age, color, sexual orientation, gender or ethnicity.

Your body is amazing and I am so happy that you've made it this far and I just want to say thank you.

Thank you. Thank you. Thank you. Thank you.

I cannot wait for you to go out into the world and be whatever ice cream flavour you are, growing your plants in your head and letting the bats out of your belfry. I should thank you for patience for the strange way to explain things, I have always been one for the road less travelled.

You can always find me on Instagram because I would love to cheer you on because a lot of people who come find me and discover body acceptance; they start posting pictures of themselves in bikinis with those beautiful bodies and they're like, "oh my God, you know what? I love my body." And I scream in the comments. I am your hype person. My job in this world is to put crowns on people's heads and support because we are all kings. All I want to do is help you put your crown back on your head and continue living the life that you deserve because you are wonderful. You are cool, amazing, special, awesome, smart and charismatic.

And I really hope the rest of your journey is a wonderful experience of trying new things and being afraid and feeling like an idiot and then posting stuff on social media and realising that actually no one really cares what everyone is actually cheering for you because we want more authenticity on social media.

The more that you put yourself out there into the world and accept who you are and the fact that is awesome and do stuff that you love, the world will become a better place.

I cannot leave you without telling you this because I believe with every ounce of my soul and Ghost Jade agrees with me and she will be sitting on your shoulder reminding you about it until you don't need her anymore.

You have a beautiful body. It is phenomenal. It is gorgeous, it is beyond outstanding. No matter what shape, size, ethnicity, colour. No Matter What. You have a beautiful body and you know what? That is the least interesting thing about you.

Go shine my beautiful dandelion. You deserve a great life.

Go get it.

Love Jade

LOVE LETTER

I want to sit and thank everyone one possible to make this happen.

First, I want to thank all the amazing men in my life who have been lessons, angels, demons and everything in between. You all taught me something. You guys are a treasure trove of human beings and I am go lucky to have known you.

I want to thank my family, the team who stuck by me when things got rough and up and down. My smart and inspirational sisters who I love so much. My mother, the winnie the pooh of the world who is my biggest fan and my Aunt, who inspires me to be kind everyday with her magic. My Brother, who always had my back and taught me so much. My Father, who gave us a great childhood. My Wife, Chloe, Dana and my inner sanctum of best friends who cheered me on. I changed your names in this book but you are all important to me. My handsome man, who supported me in so many ways. You guys all mean the world to me.

To everyone on my journey who has supported, cheered me on and believed in me. Thank. Fucking. You. This is all happening because of you. BECAUSE you were kind, this dream became a reality for me. Thank you.

To all the people who bought this book. You are so appreciative, it's unreal. I hope it makes you realise that you are DOPE as hell and you deserve all the love in your life. Thank you, you superstar! I mean what I say in this book, I mean every word.

I want to thank all the people who didn't believe in me, all those neigh sayers who told me what I had to offer was garbage. Thank you. I love a little motivation. I wish you nothing but love and light.

Humbly, I want to thank myself for being brave enough to go out and help myself. Now Jade 4.0 can help people avoid the mistakes we have made and find happiness a lot faster than we did!

Thank you and you all deserve love and peace!

Printed in Great Britain
by Amazon